Practical Ideas
for Home Decoration

LOFT

Editorial coordination: Cristina Paredes

Texts: Ana Ventura

Translation: Antonio Moreno, Jay Noden

Art director: Mireia Casanovas Soley

Layout: Ignasi Gracia Blanco

Editorial project:

2007 © **LOFT Publications**
Via Laietana 32, 4° Of. 92
08003 Barcelona, Spain
Tel.: +34 932 688 088
Fax: +34 932 687 073
loft@loftpublications.com
www.loftpublications.com

ISBN 13: 978-84-95832-67-2
ISBN 10: 84-95832-67-4

Printed in China

This books aims to be a useful compendium on home decoration based on atmospheres created by reputable artists, interior designers and decorators from around the world, while using the very latest models by international furniture makers. Directed toward the public at large, this volume offers a large amount of ideas, tricks, suggestions, advice and solutions for all those interested in decorating a home for the first time or remodeling an old house.

A well-designed interior doesn't only mean following the latest trends in interior design; it's also about reflecting its owner and their personality, highlighting their interests and tastes. Hence, interiors should grow and develop, adapting to the passing of time and our changing needs.

Practical Ideas for Home Decoration is full of spaces that speak of warm individuals, lovers of the family life, or dynamic people with an intense social life, or even sensitive and romantic people with high hopes for the near future. Today's home interiors aren't only to be displayed. They are used on a daily basis, so it's important that decorative elements are not only practical but that they meet the owners'

personal expectations and reflect the way they look at the world.

This book has been designed to be a model of inspiration for all those wishing to decorate their homes. Its pages are filled with fresh ideas and make for a well-varied source of inspiration, managing to cover the latest international trends in decoration, from the most traditional to the most avant-garde.

The book includes basic concepts for distributing space, materials, colors, styles, fabrics, furniture, accessories and lighting, with the aim of covering all the basic rules in decoration. However, when deciding upon decorating an interior, it's necessary to compare other styles and trends, even on an international level. A home should meet its owners' needs and personalities while making each and every room special. This is the only way of making a house a home.

Planning the distribution of space should be the foundation of any interior design. This doesn't only mean how you'll arrange the furniture but how the spaces will relate to each other and how one will

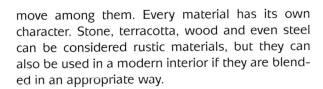

move among them. Every material has its own character. Stone, terracotta, wood and even steel can be considered rustic materials, but they can also be used in a modern interior if they are blended in an appropriate way.

The interiors that are included in the following pages cover the whole spectrum of colors, from pure white areas to those with an explosion of reds and blues, as well as spaces that make use of a limited color palette. This book also explains how colors affect one's character and how to manage combining them satisfactorily.

A large variety of styles should also be considered. Readers will be able to see modern interiors that are easily adapted, rustic homes for those where time has not passed, country styles, romantic rooms, smooth and friendly interiors alongside urban and metallic designs, homes that clearly breathe the Mediterranean style and even interesting examples of the modernist style.

Fabrics are a very attractive resource in decoration. They tend to be used for their textures, but carpets, cushions, blankets and bedspreads are often a colorful solution for a monochromatic area.

Natural light is usually controlled with curtains and blinds, playing with colors and shade. Artificial light, on the other hand, comes on to the scene with strategically placed wall lamps or small lamps giving off direct or indirect light.

Although accessories aren't always given the importance they deserve, it's evident that their presence helps achieve a certain rhythm, defining the finishing touches of one's personality: paintings, photos, plants, small objects such as cushions, jugs, etc, tend to become the center of attention while introducing color and style.

In conclusion, this book is an inexhaustible source of easy and practical information that makes for a very complete guide for the public at large. Explicative text and over 1000 color photographs help readers understand the exciting world of decoration.

Fabrics

Perhaps we don't always know how to value the decorative qualities of fabrics. Not only are they an inexpensive element, but they also allow us to change their arrangement without any additional costs. For example, think of the cover of a chair or sofa. We can arrange them differently depending on the effect we're looking for. Adding ribbons will give them a romantic look, tied strings give a natural atmosphere, arranging them in straight lines makes for a more modern and functional fin-ish... in this case, it's up to us to make the fabric just another decorative element or to give it greater importance as such.

Fabrics have endless possibilities that are only limited by our creativity and imagination. We can use them the way tradition has shown us, on the table, on the bed, on windows, as upholstery... or take advantage of their decorative power and, rather than having them merely serve as functional objects, we can lend them greater decorative importance.

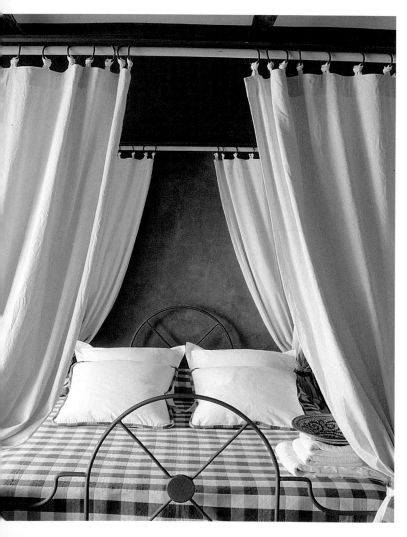

Curtains

We can use any fabric to make curtains, from fine silk or gauze to thicker fabrics such as sackcloth. If we opt for thin materials and these don't meet our needs when it comes to light and temperature, we can add a second curtain for purely functional purposes.

We must always make sure that the curtains match the atmosphere of the space where they'll be put and are coherent with the rest of the fabrics we can find in the room. We can say that any material is good for making curtains. Our choice will be determined by our budget –we remind you that when it comes to curtains we must buy twice the amount of fabric as the window we are covering– and the style we're after. Smooth and natural fabrics such as cotton give a fresh and modern feel; silks, a delicate and romantic atmosphere; thick printed cloths create period atmosphere; sackcloth suggests more rustic styles... How you place the fabric is as important as the fabric itself, and this is determined by the curtain rod itself and how it hangs from it. The choice of one type or another will determine the style we're after.

Roman blinds

Roll-up blinds

Venetian blinds

Lace curtains

Roman blinds

Very popular in recent years, roman blinds are very practical decorative elements and clearly reflect contemporary esthetics. They can be used alone or in combination with other types of curtains and can be taken up at different heights. They can be made from any material and made to fit any size, although you can also find standard sizes in basic colors on the market. They work with strips that are hidden in the cloth and which are gathered by a system of strings forming horizontal folds at the desired height. Although they are more difficult to make than curtains and must be made by a specialist, they tend to be less expensive because they require less cloth. When choosing the material we want to make them with we must be careful that the print is not too large because, once folded, the image will be interrupted and we won't achieve the desired effect.

Roman blinds give a room a sense of unity, enabling us to combine fabrics with different prints.

Do

- Combine fabrics that share the same tones, whether they are plain or printed.

- Use in small spaces since Roman blinds and roll-ups take up less space and give off a greater sense of spaciousness.

- Use in rooms with large windows, combining different types of curtains such as Roman blinds, lace curtains... making them more complex.

Don't

- Decorate a small room with lots of different prints and colors. This reduces its dimensions and makes it look disorganized.

- Use large prints when making Roman blinds, since these can't be appreciated when folded.

- Combine different prints of different colors. We can combine them if they are of the same tone or combine the tones when the print is the same.

Roll-up blinds

While they look similar to Roman blinds, roll-ups use a more simple system. Plain cloth is rolled from the top of the blinds with a system of strings. They are very useful in serving as net curtains, since they provide intimacy while allowing light to pass. Just like Roman blinds, their height can be regulated depending on our needs; we can find them on the market in standard sizes but they can also be made to measure. Traditionally, roll-up blinds gather at the top of the window, but today they also make models where the fabric rolls at the bottom, creating a screen effect.

And while looking similar to Roman blinds, roll-up blinds allow us to pick up the fabric from above or below, giving us the possibility of setting their height depending on our needs.

Venetian blinds

Can be made from wood, metal, fabric or plastic, although fabric gives the warmest finish. They consist of vertical or horizontal strips with a system that allows one to regulate their inclination while adjusting their opening. This type of composition gives the windows, and the rooms they are located in, a great esthetic quality.

Venetian blinds allow us to regulate light by inclining the slats while adjusting height by raising or lowing them.

With a modern and functional look, Venetian blinds adapt well to spaces with simple and clean lines. They can also be put between the two glass windowpanes of an insulation window, which keeps them from getting filthy.

Lace curtains

We can use thin materials such as gauze, muslin, cambric (batiste) and even shiny fabrics like silk or organdie to make lace curtains. Their purpose is to adjust the passage of light without acting as a barrier. We can also use them with a decorative effect forming effective drapes giving a room a romantic mood.

By using color fabrics the light that comes through the window will acquire a tone that helps give a space atmosphere. We can make lace curtains as we would regular curtains, but we can also try new effects with drapes, or by tensing the fabric over a rigid frame, or by using any other systems at our disposition.

The main purpose of lace curtains is to diffuse light, while at the same time giving a space a special atmosphere.

When combined with curtains they can create very effective drapes.

Upholstery

Upholstery helps us change the look of our furniture at a low cost, keeping in mind that good upholstery can last many years. We'll decide if it's better to reupholster an old piece of furniture or substitute it for a new one by objectively analyzing the value of the furniture. If we are doubtful between one option and the other, or if we want a more economical solution, we'll opt to cover the furniture with the fabric of our choice, fixing it down if necessary. This makes for an effective and economic solution that solves the problem quickly, even if for only a short time.

High quality upholstery fabrics tend to be expensive, although the market offers a great variety of types and prices. We must consider the amount of material necessary to upholster the furniture, since a few meters can greatly affect the total price. Not only must you take the price of the material into account, but also how to place it. We can judge the quality of a given material by its weight, a characteristic that indicates its durability. This is calculated by submitting the fabric to friction: high quality means the material won't change over a considerable time period. We can also use materials that aren't expressly intended to serve as upholstery, but later we may find ourselves with problems such as wrinkles.

The choice of color or print is very important. We must understand that not only must it match the curtains, but also the rest of the furniture and the color of the floors and walls. If it's difficult to choose or we're not sure of ourselves, we can choose neutral colors, especially beige and gray, which tend to match well with any color. If we prefer a printed fabric, stripes with neutral colors are the best choice for adapting to all spaces, styles and atmospheres. When choosing we must also consider the purpose of the furniture we are upholstering. If it must handle being treated by careless people such as children, we'll choose dark colors and fabrics that are prepared to handle filth and stains. If we are upholstering a sofa that will be near the chimney we should use non-flammable materials, or if will be placed outdoors it should be able to handle humidity and direct light exposure. Specialists will help us choose the upholstery that best adapts to our needs. Silk and chintz are not advisable materials since they are too fine and delicate. Cotton, linen and light wool are great materials for making covers since they are easy to wash, although they aren't very resistant to time, so we should avoid using them as upholstery. Indian cotton, velvet and washed denim are strong and solid materials that give very good results. Generally speaking, the thicker and more close-woven a fabric, and the more body it has, the better it will handle friction and time; making them better for upholstery.

To give upholstery a more personal finishing touch we can add buttons covered in cloth or sewn borders. We can also play with combining the upholstery print with that of the cushions to create playful color combinations.

Upholstery lends warmth to the space it's decorating while changing the look of a piece of furniture in a simple and economical way.

Carpets

Carpets are elements that give countless decorative possibilities. They allow us to convert a hard, cold stone floor into a warm and cozy floor that is pleasant to the feet. They are ideal for unifying spaces in living areas by creating delimiting atmospheres, making a reception area or a staircase an area of interest in itself, becoming a place where one can sit or lie down at informal reunions... not to mention they are a decorative element that lends esthetic quality to a room. We have to ignore the popular belief that carpets are expensive. If we look at kilims or imported carpets or those that are made to measure, surely the prices will be high, but we can also find affordable carpets on the market.

We should remember that they are of great durability and adapt to different spaces, can be moved from one room to another and even from one home to another when we move. It's important to place carpets correctly, on a level floor, keeping them from getting wrinkled. If the floor we are putting the carpet on is slippery we can fix it by putting a rubber fabric beneath it to keep the carpet from shifting.

A brief review of the different types and styles of carpets will help us distinguish them and decide which adapts best to the atmosphere we're creating:

Oriental. Thick and heavy with artistic content, they come from China in colors like yellow, black, peach, blue and pink. Today they are made in countries where manual labor is cheap, such as India,

making them more economical. They are made in wool or silk.

Kilims. They are made in Iran, Iraq, China, Pakistan, India, Russia and Morocco. They come in many different styles depending on the tribes and regions where they are made, so they come in a large variety of colors and motifs. They are thick and somewhat rough, and elongated pieces are more prized than those that are largest.

Persian. We can find them rectangular or elongated, all of them made in knitted wool, so their appearance improves over time. Red and blue are the colors that predominate in their designs.

Turkmen carpets. Easy to distinguish because they have small, repetitive geometric patterns. They come from Pakistan and Afghanistan. They aren't very resistant and are not very recommendable for areas with a lot of traffic. Small pieces are more valuable because of their greater amount of detail work.

Dhurry rugs. Made in India, they come in a large variety of colors and sizes. They are made of cotton, making them better for the summer than the winter.

Others. We can find other types of carpets that are not as known and common, such as the Caucasian ones, which are colorful, with borders and childish motifs; those made of rags, made by joining pieces of cloth; flokati, from Greece, which are heavy and hairy; rya, from the Nordic countries, with fringes and long hair, and sarape, blankets from Mexico or Turkey.

A bright and colorful carpet will lend playful character to a neutral space.

Carpets with small and repetitive prints are ideal for areas with straight and simple lines.

- Use carpets to lend greater warmth and comfort to spaces with hard or cold floors.

- Carpet delicate floors that must handle a lot of traffic. They make walking more comfortable while protecting the floor.

- Choose the curtains according to our functional needs, while keeping in mind the style we're looking for.

- Abuse prints by combining curtains, upholstery and carpets in an overloaded style.

- Plan and choose your fabrics separately since the end result will not be unified.

- Choose delicate fabrics for upholstering sofas that are going to be used regularly.

L'AFRIQUE
des années 50 ...
rencontre
L'AMÉRIQUE
des années 90 !

Top 10 Tips

1 Combine the fabrics of the curtains and upholstery to unify spaces that look disorganized.

2 Use carpets as elements for delimiting space. A carpet is ideal for creating a gathering area with sofas and armchairs around it.

3 Fabrics with classic prints are very adequate for creating period atmospheres.

4 Bear in mind that sheets, blankets and towels also form part of the decoration and should also be in tune.

5 Thin fabrics such as gauzes, nets and laces allow us to diffuse light.

6 Use versatile curtains such as Venetian blinds for spaces in need of variable light such as study areas.

7 Do not limit curtain use to windows. Roman blinds can serve as folding screens, curtains will help us divide a hallway that is too long, the way that a door would...

8 In rooms with a lot of paintings, different color walls and different color furniture is more advisable than neutral curtains and upholstery.

9 Take advantage of the possibilities that fabrics offer when combining the look of your furniture and making covers for them.

10 Use carpets and upholstery as if they were paintings. Their color is unmatchable and they provide warmth and acoustic quality to a space.

Flooring

Flooring is understood as all those materials that are used to cover a floor.

Further ahead we will look at the importance of the walls as a consequence of the surface area they take up, but the floors, although they take up a smaller surface, are just as important. We must not only look at their esthetic look. Their importance is also due to the fact that we are in constant contact with them, so they can directly influence our comfort.

Choosing a floor can be a complicated task. There is more than one adequate material for every purpose. We must choose the one that best suits our needs and our budget, without forgetting that it must match the general atmosphere of the home and, more specifically, the atmosphere we're decorating. We must also consider the characteristics of the building since some types of flooring are very heavy or require a very heavy base and are not suitable for old homes or those with damaged structures that can't handle considerable weight. It's also important to keep in mind that there will be points where the different types of flooring will meet, creating unions that can be tricky to solve. We'll try to make sure there aren't too many unions in areas like the hallway or the reception, since these tend to be connecting points to many areas. The joining of different types of flooring can give unattractive results that we must think about upon choosing our material.

Wood

It's probably one of the first and oldest construction materials. Wood comes from live matter and this gives it a special character that other materials do not have. Its variety of colors and patterns offer an endless array of decorative possibilities. Its natural heritage makes it grow older over time. Careful maintenance will keep it unchanged for many years, although in some cases it might interest us to exploit the character wood acquires over time since its patina is as attractive as that of old furniture.

The characteristics that define wood are its color, tone, density, texture, knots and grain. But its possibilities don't quite finish here since the market offers a large array of varieties: strips, plywood, conglomerated in different densi-ties, boards and even high quality imitations like melamine.

The size of the pieces and their arrangement will also be determining factors when creating a space. Smaller pieces give a fuller look that is more heterogeneous than those made with large pieces, which give off an air of spaciousness.

Wood can handle a large number of treatments that we can first experiment with a few trials. Bleaching, lacquering, oil treatment, painting, staining, and varnishing are some of the most common treatments. You have to keep in mind that wood has a base color that can change the tone we want to apply on top of it. The same thing occurs when we use varnish or stains. In addition, light and time change the color of wood, so we should protect it from

Parquet

Strips

Tessellated pavements

Wood finishes

direct sunlight and move the furniture and carpets that cover it to keep unattractive light stains from developing.

Wood provides flooring halfway between that of rigid and flexible materials while offering the advantages of both of them. It responds positively to acoustics, since it absorbs noise, while at the same time being a noisy element in itself. We might find that long strips of wood can produce annoying sounds for those living on the floor below. A proper installation with elements that cushion sound, such as felt or carpets are an effective solution. Solid wood can be restored, making it possible that it last a long time when cared for properly. Veneered floors are undoubtedly more economical but, since they don't allow for restorations, their life will be shorter. We must always remember that wood is a particularly delicate material that requires special treatment, and we should avoid putting it in places where they might be treated carelessly, such as areas that are near the outdoors. In these areas, carpets should be used to protect the wood from direct contact with filthy shoes. Wood should be varnished periodically to protect it from further damage.

Its warmth makes it an adequate material for all kinds of spaces. Temperature changes and humidity easily affect it, so it's important that we treat it properly when putting it in areas like the kitchen or bathroom so it handles the conditions better.

Wood is sold prepared for installation. For this it must have undergone a drying process. This doesn't prevent it from suffering great changes after it has been placed. In any case, if we're going to put the wood in a space with humidity or special temperatures it's advisable that we leave the wood in that place for a period of one or two months so it can adapt to the conditions. This assures us that once placed it won't undergo great changes: contractions, expansions or even cracks. Installing wood in strips or floor tiles, sometimes with borders and motifs that repeat, lends rhythm to a space. In these cases we must decide on the ori-

entation we want to emphasize since, depending on how they are placed, it can highlight one direction or another. In elongated rooms, placing strips parallel to the longest side accentuates this direction, making the room seem even longer than it is. We'll achieve the opposite effect if we place them perpendicular to it.

Decoration is the art with which we take advantage of all the resources offered us by materials, giving a room its character. For example, in a hallway we might want to emphasize direction, and choose to arrange the strips parallel to the longest side despite its elongated nature.

Growing interest in ecological and natural products has made wood increasingly more popular. We must make sure the wood comes from a sustainable plantation, especially when it comes to tropical woods (iroko, sapelly, teak and keruing) since it's prohibited from

exporting some of them due to the heavy forest exploitation going on in these areas. We should also make sure that the products we use to treat the wood, such as varnishes, paints and primers are as natural as possible.

The final look and result depends on the way it is cut. Cutting wood with its grain gives a wood that is harder than when cut radially, even if cutting it radially gives a wood with a more uniform finish as far as grain is concerned. Lastly, it can be cut straight, a more economical method that is more common, even if the wood is of lesser quality since it proves less resistant over time.

A wood's density is another characteristic to bear in mind. The denser they are the more resistant they are, and the better they handle damage and time. The different types of wood can be divided in two large groups. Noble or hard wood is more resistant, more expensive and varied. Soft or coniferous wood is less resistant, cheaper and more abundant. These days hard woods are used more often, whether solid or veneered, which explains why there's a greater variety of them on the market with different finishes, textures and motifs.

The woods that are most often used as flooring are:

Beech. Light-colored, resistant and very durable.

Ash. Rough texture, light-colored and irregular shape.

Maple. Red-colored, very resistant.

Oak. Resistant, solid and durable.

Irregular grain. Widely used for its resistance against humidity and pests.

There are also other types of wood that are lesser known as they are less frequently used: birch, of delicate texture and light-colored; chestnut, resistant and durable; cherry, of fine grain and pinkish color; lime, light-colored with straight grain; walnut, of wavy grain; elm, dark-colored and resistant; sycamore, light-colored. Pine is a soft and light wood, not very resistant, but often used as it is more economical.

Its possibilities are not limited to solid wood. Today's technology has developed types of wood such as plywood and melamine, which offer a world of possibilities at a more economical price. Plywood is based on various layers of wood joined with glue and pressed, arranged so the grain goes in different directions with each layer. They can be formed by layers of the same noble wood or using noble wood for the finish and soft wood for the inner layers. Melamine is formed with a board of agglomerate particles inside and a finish formed by a fine layer of melamine paper that imitates the look of different woods. The base of the agglomerated particles is a mass of wood particles stuck together with glue.

Modern designs are using conglomerated wood much more frequently, often with no other protection than a natural wood style coat of varnish. We'll find different types of conglomerated wood depending on the material they're made of. The result is smooth and uniform when they are made with wood fiber. This type of conglomerate is also known as MDF. The conglomerates most widely used are made with tiny wood scraps. There are also conglomerates made from larger pieces, giving a texture with a richer and more attractive finish.

Although it demands care that other materials don't, wood responds well to time and becomes more beautiful, acquiring a patina that gives it its special character.

Do	Don't
• Choose the type of wood depending on its purpose and the space where it will be placed. • Analyze what kind of placement and arrangement best adapts to the space's decoration and atmosphere. • Give wood that will be exposed to special humidity conditions the proper protective treatment.	• Abuse wood placing it on floors, walls, ceilings... unless the decorative atmosphere we're creating demands it. • Use wood in spaces that will be exposed to a lot of traffic, direct contact with the outdoors, high humidity... • Use small pieces of wood to decorate large areas. Long and wide strips are better for this.

Parquet

Currently very popular, it was also widely known and used in French palaces in the XVII and XVIII centuries. Parquet can be installed in different ways, but generally speaking, strips are nailed into small bases in the form of small beams placed perpendicularly with one or two-foot separations between them, which are used to level the floor. A layer of flexible felt isolates the material from humidity that might affect the floor base, which is usually concrete or cement. Sand can be placed between the beams to assure a good acoustic response. You can also place some flexible felt between the strips and the beams to cushion the sound of footsteps and that of the wood itself.

Simpler and more complex placement variations have emerged to address more specific needs. Specialists will inform us as to which placement best adapts to our needs. On the other hand, we find a large variety of finishes that not only depend on the type of wood, but also on the size of the strips and their placement, which can range from the most simple linear arrangements to the most complex arrangements of diamond shapes, motifs and borders

Aside from the traditional parquet installation methods that should be done by a specialist, the market offers us other more simple systems that can be installed by anyone with basic DIY knowledge; we're talking about parquet with veneered wood (not solid as before) that can be bought ready for installation and which normally don't need any previous floor preparation with beams or other elements.

Parquet is made of noble wood, although often pine is used as well.

The traditional installation process is tedious and should be done by a specialist if we want the result to be on par with the beauty a material such as wood is capable of.

Do

- Give parquet a special treatment when installing it in bathrooms and kitchens.

- Use long and wide strips in large areas and small ones in smaller spaces.

- Leave expansion joints where the parquet meets the wall to leave room for the wood's natural movement.

Don't

- Place parquet in places that are in direct contact with the outdoors, since filthy shoes will destroy it.

- Use parquet on floors with high levels of humidity.

- Place it in areas of high traffic or friction. If we do it, it's best if we protect it with a carpet.

Strips

Installing these kinds of floors is similar to parquet, although the end result can be quite different. The size of the strips can vary, in length and in width, as well as their price. The wider and the longer, the more expensive they'll be. Width varies between 8 and 25 mm (0.31 and 0.98 inches) and whether or not it can be restored depends on this width since it requires sanding that will take away from its width. We should also make sure that the dovetail joints are not affected by this reduction. Wider strips give a more elegant and luxurious finish, although sometimes they're not as appropriate, especially in smaller spaces where they can't reach their maximum expression. In this case we also find prefabricated solutions on the market that are easy to install and are less expensive.

Wood strips make a space more linear, making them ideal for emphasizing direction.

Tessellated pavements

Tessellated pavements are less common since their finish isn't as elegant. They are made of tiles consisting of small strips forming a geometric drawing or motif. Just like other wood floors, they come in different sizes and widths, and have various methods of installation, using either adhesive tape stuck to the floor or dovetail joints joining the tiles.

Wood finishes

We can color a wood with paint or stains. Wood acquires a smooth finish that hides its natural look, so you can't see its knots and grain. Generally speaking, this type of finish doesn't handle friction and traffic well, so it should be limited to areas with less traffic. Types of paints that are most suitable for wood are enamels, which leave a shiny finish; semi-matte paints, with a less shiny finish; and those with epoxy resin that are more resistant. Painting gives us other possibilities such as stripping and decorative motifs. We can also strip the floor the same way we strip furniture, so you can see the grain and knots. In addition to this, painting offers a world of possibilities when treating wood with decorative motifs. We shouldn't be afraid when experimenting with the great possibilities wood has to offer. In any case, it's very useful and advisable to first practice a few trial runs on the wood.

Staining allows for a less radical treatment than painting. Wood that will be stained must first be treated with a layer of primer that makes it watertight, before going on to stain the wood carefully to avoid different tones. If you begin by bleaching the wood you'll be able to obtain lighter tones. There are different types of stain bases: water, oil or turpentine. Professionals will inform us which is best for our needs and the wood we're about to treat.

Do

- Choose harder woods for areas that will be exposed to heavy traffic.

- The strips mark the direction of the space. We should take advantage of this quality to make narrow rooms seem wider, and short ones longer.

- Let the wood sit for a few days in the room where it's going to be placed so it can adjust to the climate conditions.

Don't

- Wash the parquet with abundant water or corrosive chemical products.

- Use parquet in areas where the furniture is often moved because these floors get scraped easily.

- Paint or stain a parquet that has first been varnished. This treatment can only be applied to natural wood.

Hard flooring

A wide variety of highly resistant and durable materials fit into this category. This group encompasses bricks, ceramic floors, stone, marble, earthenware floors... All of them give elegant, but cold, results. Their great resistance makes them adequate for all kinds of spaces, including those that are more in contact with the outdoors. But before choosing one of them we should consider a few things. First of all, they require a specialist to install them and sometimes require the base to be prepared before laying the floor.

The cost of these types of floors is usually higher, because of the price of the material itself, as well as its installation. We should also consider that these floors give a cold and hard effect (since they're not a flexible material), so they won't be appropriate for places where people walk a lot or walk barefoot. Their acoustic behavior is not so great either since they amplify sound. Nor is it a good idea to put them in buildings that are in a degraded state since they greatly increase the weight resting on the beams.

But these materials offer a world of possibilities that we should take advantage of. The colors they come in are always natural tones because of the materials that are used to make them and they give cozy results. Pieces with figurative motifs open us to a world of decoration that can adapt to a variety of spaces.

Brick

Tiles

Stone

Terrazzo

Others

Brick

Brick is, together with wood and stone, one of the oldest construction materials. Less expensive than stone, brick has been the construction element of choice amongst the poorer classes for centuries, while the affluent continued using stone to build their palaces. This origin, tied to its natural character, makes brick a warm element that separates it from the luxurious nature of stone and marble. Its rustic character makes it ideal for country cottages and mountain huts. It's particularly well-suited for ground floors and outdoors, since its weight makes it inappropriate for higher floors.

Bricks used as flooring are not the same as construction bricks. They are baked at high temperatures, making them highly resistant. Their width varies depending on the producer, model and the geographical area. In some countries we find specific types of bricks and ways of installation which we will take into account when deciding. Finishes, textures and colors also vary greatly. Hand-made bricks are harder to install, but they produce welcome rustic results that few materials can match. On the other hand, we'll be surprised by its high resistance and durability: brick is waterproof, resistant to aggression and stains, as well as easy to clean. Its ability to maintain temperature makes it perfect for having a cool floor in the summer and a warm one in the winter, especially if we have floor heating. A specialist must install these types of floors, since they must consider aspects such as expansion joints. Not to mention that only a specialist will achieve the kind of regularity that is crucial for these types of floors to be attractive. We should understand that a floor like this can last many years, even a lifetime, so despite their high cost, they'll pay for themselves.

Since they are natural, bricks give room a rustic air that is warm at the same time.

Brick finishes, textures and colors vary greatly. Natural materials, such as bricks, produce irregular results that are very attractive.

Tiles

It's difficult to speak about the different types of tiles we can find in the market, because there are many, and these vary greatly depending on the culture and tradition where we live. We find them with a wide variety of finishes, vitrified, non-vitrified, made by hand or machine... Just like bricks, they are made of natural materials such as earth, giving them a warm, textural look that acquires character over the years. However, unlike brick, tiles offer a world of color combinations and infinite decorative styles. On the other hand, they also share properties such as their hardness and coldness, making them inadequate for more personal rooms. Carpets will allow us to enjoy the benefits of tiles or bricks while providing us with a warm and cozy floor.

Professionals should install tiles if we want esthetic and long-lasting results. Their cost varies. Some models and finishes can be very economical, others too expensive. When laying tile floors we should consider that the price of the material is calculated by square meters (or feet), and you have to add installation costs on top of it. This depends on the size of the tiles beings placed since small ones require more time and attention. When we're dealing with these types of materials we must be careful transporting them since they can be very fragile and pieces that break must be replaced, raising the final cost. Besides, we should make sure to buy a few extra pieces in case some of them break over the years, this way they can be replaced.

Tile use is appropriate for lots of spaces, although traditionally they have been used most in kitchens and bathrooms. In these rooms we should take into account that some tiles are slippery when wet. They can also be appropriate in living rooms and other rooms where

Tiles are ideal for areas where we use water and food since they can be cleaned easily. Besides, they offer us a world of decorative possibilities since they allow for different combinations.

they'll look fresh and elegant. The size of the pieces should be proportional to that of the room. We must avoid large sizes in small bathrooms since they won't shine with all their splendor. Likewise, using small pieces in large rooms can produce a repetitive effect that is not esthetically pleasing. Pieces used on floors are thicker than those used for walls, which are thinner and lighter. The thickest ones provide the resistance necessary to withstand the weight and damage that a floor is exposed to. The types of tiles that are most popular and known are ceramic, terracotta, non-vitrified and encaustic floor tiles.

Ceramic tiles are resistant and uniform in color, made with refined earth that's been compressed. Vitrified tiles don't respond well to water, and we'll find some models on the market that are made with silicon carbide, which is non-slip. In addition we'll find finishes that are smooth or with granulated or fluted motifs that can also be slippery. All ceramics, and especially those that are glazed, give a clean and uniform result that is more adequate for modern spaces with simple lines. The texture and repetition of the motifs will make the floor more interesting.

Terracotta offers lots of possibilities. It offers a natural, warm and textured finish. We can find them in countless tones that vary depending on how they were made and how long they baked as well as the type of fire used. They can be made by hand or machine, but by hand is always more expensive. We can also find restored terracotta but in these cases the price will be even higher. Due to the natural material they are made of and the baking process, terracotta's irregularity makes it ideal for rustic spaces or the mountains. The warmth and elegance they provide make them a good choice for a variety of areas. Some come in tones that are pinkish, others that

are more ochre, and others that mix different tones with attractive results. In any case, we should waterproof the tiles to keep stains from damaging them. This base will darken their color slightly. They offer us a variety of shapes, sizes and thicknesses, some of them even form attractive decorative motifs by joining four or five pieces, and we can even resort to combining different tones to give the floor more decorative character.

Non-vitrified tiles are made by pressing and baking silicon-rich clay. We can also find them in vitrified finishes, although originally they were without vitrifying. They are resistant but they can feel the passage of time by their lack of a vitrified finish. Just like terracotta, they come in a range of natural colors that go from brown to beige or red. We can also find pieces that have had coloring added, achieving darker tones such as navy blue, but always very natural colors. They are adequate for interior use as well as for exteriors, since they are less slippery than tiles when they come into contact with water.

Encaustic tiles, also known as tessellated pavements because of their decorative motifs, require a more complicated production process, making them more expensive. The finish for these types of floors is matte and regular and their color changes slightly over time. Colors lose strength and white may turn yellow. They should be sealed properly to keep them from getting stained. They were frequently used in the XXth century. We can find lots of them in antique and restoration shops, and even beneath newer floors in old houses. Uncovering these kinds of floors undoubtedly adds architectural value to the home, and although it can be expensive we should consider it whenever possible.

Tessellated floors usually prese very elaborate decorative motif making them the center of attentic wherever they are placed.

Do	Don't
• Give terracotta a waterproof treatment to keep it from getting stained.	• Use heavy floors in old buildings since you can overloa them with weight.
• Use non-slip tiles in spaces that come in contact with water, such as showers.	• Use indoor flooring outdoors. They will be slippery ar they break easily.
• Save some tiles in case some of them break in the future and must be replaced.	• Choose large tiles for small areas and small tiles for larg areas.

Stone

If we highlighted the natural char-acter of terracotta, stone repre-sents nature in itself. Construction material since the origins of humanity, we find it in majestic buildings such as castles and cathe-drals, but also in more humble con-structions such as homes and farms. The many finishes, colors, shapes and textures they present open us to a world of possibilities, to be used for floors as well as for other surfaces. Typically, stone fin-ishes can be polished, refined, slightly worked or rough. Their thickness depends on the resist-ance of a given stone. Their weight demands that you prepare the floor with a regulating layer of concrete, making it inadequate for apart-ments.

We can buy the stone in specialized stores or at the quarries them-selves, and we must also have a specialist install them since they are very delicate. It's hard to find a material that matches its character; it's impossible to find two pieces that are alike. They are appropriate for all kinds of spaces, but in this case we must also make sure that the size of the slabs are proportion-al to the dimensions of the space. A stone-covered hall will provide an elegance that will be difficult to match with any other material.

There are many types of stones that we can find on the market and they depend on the area where we are. Generally speaking, stones are classified depending on whether they come from metamorphic, sed-imentary or igneous rocks. Meta-morphic rocks have been formed by high temperature and pressure, making them very hard. Marble and slate are the most popular stones in this group. Sedimentary rocks are made of sediments and organic matter, are less resistant and have a more textural finish. In this group we can find sandstone and lime-

Stone gives a very natural and irreg ular finish. We'll never find two piece that are alike, making the spaces the decorate unique.

stone, widely used in construction. Lastly, igneous rocks are the oldest and have shiny finishes on account of their crystalline nature. Granite is the most popular igneous rock. We can also find old stones coming from old buildings. In this case we should check out where they are from and make sure they are not stones of artistic or architectural value.

Granite is resistant, hard and waterproof, so it responds well to the aggression of chemical products. It consists of a feldspar, quartz and mica compound. Granite's finish will depend on how it will be used. It can be slippery when it comes into contact with water, so we must give it a rough finish if we are to place it in the kitchen or bathroom. Time and traffic can polish the material and diminish its rough finish. If this occurs you'll have to have a profes-

sional treat it and bring back its original finish.

Limestone usually offers smoother colors and tones than granite, although we can also find it in darker colors, devoid of the liveliness provided by granite's crystalline nature. Limestone is more economical than granite, but it's also less resistant. It doesn't handle time as well and doesn't handle the most common chemical products. Sandstone falls halfway between granite and limestone. More resistant than the latter, and more economical as well. However, its porosity makes it less resistant than granite.

Marble is the most popular and valued stone, perhaps on account of its role throughout history. Used ad nauseam and often imitated, it has lost the value it held throughout the XXth century, although contemporary design is bringing it

back in its purest form. Marble offers a wide range of colors, from the most purest of whites or black, passing through a range of greens, blues, and pinks... The types of marble we might find depend on where we live. We can also find imported marble which is more expensive, the most famous of which being that of Italy, which is of great quality. Purity is determined by its lack of imperfections and remains of other minerals, meaning that the purest marble is that which doesn't have any grain. Curiously, these are not the most valued, since the grain is what gives this material its character. We can find it in finishes that are very similar to that of the other stones. But we can't use it anyplace we want because it may seem too classical or cold.

Slate, which comes from mountainous regions, comes in a variety of tones that are always dark but with attractive and delicate touches. We can find them in ranges of gray, violet, blue and red and with

finishes that can be serrated or polished. More economical than marble and granite, it is impermeable and resistant, in addition to demanding little maintenance.

We can also find less common types of stone floors such as cobble or pebble, more often used outdoors but which can also be very interesting to use indoors. The market also offers possibilities such as artificial stones. On one hand we find those that are made using agglomerations of stone pieces that give a varied and irregular look. Some types, made with stone powder, can have homogenous finishes.

On the other hand, we can find concrete treated with paint or other materials, to create a look similar to stone. Despite the existence of accurate reproductions, it's better to avoid these types of materials since they usually aren't very effective. An exception being cases where we are looking for falsity for decorative or theatric purposes.

Although polished stone is the mo popular finish, since it is shiny ar regular, a more natural finish lenc texture, warmth and naturalness to space.

Do

- Treat porous stones with an impermeable substance to keep them from getting stained.

- Give the stone a rough finish when used as outdoor flooring, or if in contact with water, to keep them from being slippery.

Don't

- Use stone floors in areas where people will walk barefoo since they are cold and hard. If we choose to do so w should use carpets to make them more comfortable.

- White marble is porous and stains easily, and the stair don't disappear by polishing it, so we should avoid using in areas like the kitchen.

Terrazzo

Terrazzo is widely used for its resistance and durability, its reasonable price and the quality of its finish. It is made with pieces of marble or conglomerated granite stuck together with cement or concrete. Esthetically, the result depends on the size of the pieces and the coloring used to join the materials. We can find pieces presenting geometric shapes that are very adequate for modern atmos-pheres. They can also be made on-site, giving a continuous finish that is very appropriate for public spaces. In this case, it can be arranged to form geometric drawings or motifs. It is placed using thin metallic strips that are removed afterwards. We can decide to incorporate these tin or zinc metal strips into the design to delimit areas with different colors and help shape motifs.

Terrazzo is widely used for its marble appearance at lower cost.

Others

Materials such as concrete, metal or glass are not so frequently used because they are not as popular. Their finishes, which are especially adequate for modern spaces and atmospheres, are of great esthetic quality. While concrete can look too industrial, it allows for lots of treatments that can change its image, such as painting, plaster, waxing or even texturing, giving it a quality finish that is also very attractive.

Aluminum and galvanized steel are the materials most used as floors. We can find them in the shape of tiles or sheets, most of them textured with geometric motifs to keep them from being slippery. In humid areas we might opt for aluminum since it doesn't rust. The sheets of metal or tiles are applied with glue or they are nailed into a wood or concrete base, though wood is preferable because you obtain greater flexibility and warmth.

Glass is not as used because of its high cost, but it does present a luxurious and spectacular finish. The glass pieces or tiles are joined with neoprene rubber and the finish must be treated to give it texture since it can be extremely slippery. Thick tempered glass is best for this because it is resistant and can withstand weight. We'll consult a specialist about how thick the glass should be for the space where we'll be putting it.

Waxed concrete acquires a very esthetic shiny look that enables it to be used in all kinds of spaces.

Textile floors

While textile floors are very warm, they are not very often used on account of their low resistance to traffic and the filth that comes along with it. Contemporary decoration esthetics are slowly bringing them back for their natural value. While fitted carpets are widely used in cold countries, they are a long way from the trends in Mediterranean design. On the other hand, natural fibers are developing at an unstoppable pace and are taking over many of the areas in our homes. Carpets, which we already looked at in the chapter devoted to fabrics, forms part of this group of warm, natural and comfortable floors. Placing textile floors is somewhat complicated, although when it's done correctly you can be guaranteed long-lasting durability without wrinkles. In any case, we must be careful with stains since they are very difficult to clean. It's advisable to apply a treatment that protects against filth.

Natural fibers

Fitted carpets

Natural fibers

Natural fiber floor and carpets made of coconut or seaweed are being used in contemporary design since they are comfortable, fresh, contemporary and economical materials. Among the most known natural fibers we'll find jute –soft and not durable–, coconut and sisal –which are rougher–, seaweed and reed.

Coconut is available in different types of fabric such as herringbone or diamond. It's rough and course, making it especially good for rustic atmospheres. We can also find it in dyed finishes and in fabrics that combine different colors.

Seaweed gives a smoother finish, while being cleaner thanks to its impermeability. On the other hand, we can only find it in its natural color since it doesn't accept dyes. It is good for all kinds of spaces, as long as it doesn't have to withstand high humidity levels.

Jute can also be found in different tones, though these are always more whitish. It has a soft finish, but it's less resistant to traffic and stains, so it's advisable to apply a protective treatment.

Reed, which looks like coconut only rougher, is very resistant. One of its advantages is that it can be placed in humid spaces since it needs a certain level of humidity to retain its natural properties.

However, **sisal** is the most known of all the natural fibers. With a final finish that's in between soft and rough, it adapts to all spaces and situations. We can also find it different tones, but it should receive treatment to protect it against stains and filth.

Natural fibers can also be used on surfaces, since we can find them on the market in sizes big enough to cover an entire wall. In this case it is necessary to have it placed by a specialist since it's a complicated and delicate process.

Fibers provide a natural and moder finish that is rough at times. They ar delicate materials, especially wit regards to humidity.

Fitted carpets

Though fitted carpets are rarely used in warmer areas, in Nordic areas and colder regions they are a basic element for decoration and comfort. Not only do fitted carpets provide a soft and flexible floor that is pleasant to the feet, but it's also a material offering very interesting esthetic possibilities. The continuous look it acquires –the joints are hidden– allows us to unify spaces while separating them, and its wide range of colors, finishes and textures opens us to a world of possibilities in design. When choosing a fitted carpet we must bear in mind that it is a fixed floor that can last a long time if it is cared for properly, so it should easily adapt to the different decorative styles that will come about over that time. In addition to its esthetic

advantages, it is also good for thermal and acoustic insulation. It is good for any part of the home but it is not very recommendable for humid areas. One of its disadvantages is that it's easy for it to get filthy and it's difficult to clean, making it not very hygienic as far as floors are concerned.

When choosing a fitted carpet we must consider its characteristics: texture, fiber content, how it is made, weight, hair density, color and design. We'll use hair weight as a guide for choosing since it is related to its resistance as a carpet. The greater, the more resistant, and hence it will be more adequate for areas that are used more. When using carpets on surfaces it is better to choose those of lighter weight, which are easier to lay.

Carpets are appropriate in bedrooms due to their warmth, tact and visual aspect.

Do

- Vacuum textile floors often to avoid dust and filth from accumulating.

- Make sure the carpet we lay on the floor was made for this purpose. Some carpets are designed to be used on walls.

- Use special adhesive for laying carpets and textile floors in spaces that are exposed to humidity.

Don't

- Use textile floors in spaces where people allergic to dust or animals live, since they collect filth easily.

- Put textile floors in spaces near chimneys. If we do it, we must make sure they are anti-flammable.

- Lay carpets and textile floors in spaces in direct contact with the outdoors or heavy traffic.

Top 10 Tips

1 If we want to make a space warmer, we'll use floors that are pleasant to touch, such as wood, fitted carpets or natural fibers.

2 When dealing with spaces with lots of traffic or contact with the outdoors, you might consider resistant materials such as stone, marble, tiles or some hard woods.

3 If we want to change the look of a room, easily, quickly and economically we can arrange the fabrics differently: some curtains, new upholstery or covers, some carpets.

4 Periodically we'll give natural floors such as wood and terracotta adequate protective treatment. They are beautiful materials but also very delicate.

5 We'll use curtains to regulate light and give atmosphere, while also serving to determine how much light we want to enter and make the space more intimate.

6 If we are looking for sobriety or to create atmospheres with a classical touch, marble is the best material to choose.

7 Tiles are clean and resistant to humidity, making them the ideal floor for bathrooms and carpets.

8 If a space seems cold we can make it warmer with curtains and carpets, combining them with our upholstery.

9 Choosing floor and surface materials should always be done while looking to obtain unity in the atmosphere we're decorating.

10 To give a more rustic feel to the areas we're decorating we'll use natural materials such as stone or wood.

Wall coverings

When we are changing a space to adapt it to our needs, we must bear in mind that the walls carry great importance. Due to the surface area they occupy and their role as dividers of spaces they become key decorative elements. They must be very present in our minds when it comes to satisfying our needs for intimacy and lighting in the different spaces.

Their visual impact is also of great importance. Apart from setting the boundaries of a room, the walls offer a world of possibilities for modifying the perception of a space. And lets not forget that ceilings fall into the same category as the walls, since they receive the same treatment.

We can also modify our perception of a space by way of colors. Warm and dark tones make a space seem smaller, cozier and more intimate. With brighter and colder colors we create a greater sense of space, they can even make a wall appear to move back. The color is the first variable to take into account when dealing with the walls, although there are two other very important ones: the design and the texture.

By considering these variables we can exploit a wall's expressive possibilities, thus giving the space we are decorating more character.

The walls, as well as having a decorative function, play an important role for thermal and sound insulation, and provide intimacy for a house's occupants. For the walls to correctly fulfill these functions they must be in good condition and free from damp. If this is not the case, we must consult a specialist to help us solve the problem. When the walls play an important role regarding thermal insulation, thicker and warmer materials are better, like wood, stucco and padded fabric. If the problem is sound insulation then textured wall coverings like stone or fabric, which reduce noise, are more advisable.

The ceilings, which are also part of this group, require different treatment. Their height, finish and the rest of the room's features are important factors in determining their treatment. High ceilings are given texture or a strong color to make them appear lower. If the room contains important elements that are meant to stand out, then the ceiling should become a background, painted in a smooth, light color. If, on the other hand, the ceiling is in itself a feature of interest due to its moldings or plasterwork, a layer of white paint will be sufficient, although we could consider painting the cornices a different color. The space itself will often determine the requirements, i.e. whether or not there are enough features of interest. If there are not, the ceiling should be made to stand out more. But let us not forget that the space as a whole is the key to the treatment of each of the elements, so we should analyze whether or not the chosen treatment for the ceiling will match with everything else. When the space in question presents shapes and volumes which are very different, the uniform treatment of the ceiling and walls will help to bring balance and unification.

Paint

Wallpaper

Fabrics

Tiles

tucco

Paint

Out of all the techniques we can apply to the walls, paint is definitely the most economical and that which gives the most surprising results. Furthermore, its effects are immediate, which allows us to introduce modifications. There are a multitude of different types of paints in specialist retailers, and the professionals will help to choose that which most suits our needs. We should not only consider the finish, but also the material we are applying it to and the conditions it will be subject to: if it will have to survive damp, if we want it to be washable... all these variables will help us to choose one type of paint over another.

Paints known as emulsions are water-based, and therefore are more easily used and faster drying, although do not last as long. Lacquers are highly resistant, giving the walls a longer life and make the walls appear brighter. For oil-based paints, there are various types: those that give gloss finishes, whether high gloss or semi-gloss porcelain enamels, which are washable and ideal for applying to wood and metal. This type of paint must be applied to walls that have no imperfections, otherwise the effect will be greatly exaggerated. Matt and gloss paints are more suitable for hiding imperfections. Paints known as temperas or which have a latex base are more natural; the colors they offer are therefore warmer and more natural. There are also paints that can create effects, like enamels, which are prepared using 2 parts turpentine essence and 1 part oil varnish added to an oil-based paint, and which offer a shiny, smart and luminous finish. By diluting water-based paints we can create an effect of transparency, leaving the color we are painting over lightly visible.

The use of paint is also appropriat in damp spaces such as the bath room, although in this case we mus apply a paint which is made espe cially for this reason.

Do

- Use materials like paint or wallpaper to change the appearance of a space rapidly and economically. These are also easily reversible applications.

- Be sure that the paint or paper chosen for the bathroom or kitchen is water-resistant.

Don't

- Use paper or paints that are not washable in spaces tha easily get dirty, such as children's rooms.

- Paint over wallpaper, as the paint will not adhere properl or will come off along with the paper.

Wallpaper

As with paint, the possibilities with paper are infinite. Wallpaper on the market has a wide variety of motifs, from flowers to borders, stars, stripes, geometric shapes... We will without doubt be able to choose a wallpaper that matches the idea we are looking for. Furthermore we can combine wallpaper with paint creating even more possibilities. The choice of paper will be determined by the atmosphere we want the space to have. In general, we should bear in mind that in large spaces, large motifs are more suitable and in small spaces, small motifs offer better results.

When hanging wallpaper the wall must be prepared beforehand. We remove the old paint or paper until we have the original base of the wall. We apply a layer of primer to seal the surface. Then we apply the adhesive to the paper and wait five minutes as the glue may make the paper expand. We can now stick the paper to the wall. It is optional to also apply adhesive to the wall. Be sure that the motifs of the different strips coincide. A broom will help to get rid of any air bubbles or creases.

There are two basic types of wallpaper, which are different depending on how they are made. The molded pattern is more expensive but more durable, as the colors remain practically unchanged. Machine-printed paper is less costly, some can be cleaned and are more resistant to ripping as they contain vinyl. White paper is also an option, which can be painted once on the wall. In this case, stencils can be bought, which make this task easier.

For creating spaces with period decor it will be easier to use wallpaper.

Do

- Be sure that the color and motifs of the paper match the color of the floor and ceiling.

- Protect the paper with a skirting board.

- Buy more paper than you need, in case of future stains or holes that need repairing.

Don't

- Use very large patterns in small spaces or small patterns i large rooms.

- Apply the paper up until the ceiling in narrow or sma rooms. The paper can reach halfway up the wall and b finished with bordering making the space seem larger.

- Hang the paper without preparing the wall beforehan Both the paper and the paint will show any bumps an may even enlarge them.

Fabrics

Fabrics give a similar result to wallpaper in terms of their decorative motifs. Their application is especially recommended in cases where we want to give a particular room sound insulation. Putting the fabric up requires a somewhat more complex procedure than that of wallpaper, although if the wall is smooth and has a perfect finish we can put fabric up in the same way as wallpaper. If, on the other hand, the wall is not very uniform, the system of applying the fabric will be different and more complex, although it would save us from having to repair the wall.

We can use any type of fabric for this purpose, although the thicker and less elastic ones will be easier to apply. The most frequent method of applying fabric is to acquire support panels on which the fabric is held using staples, which will later be hidden beneath a decorative border. Putting the fabric onto the panels must be done very carefully to avoid creases forming and to assure that the motifs coincide. We could insert cushioning or stuffing between the fabric and the support to increase its capacity of sound absorption and to achieve a cozier finish.

The application of fabric instead of wallpaper offers a high quality, and very homely finish, although a somewhat delicate one.

Do

- Use fabric, (cushioned is better) to deaden sound.

- Assure that the colors and motifs on the fabric like with bedspreads and tablecloths match with the curtains, the paper or the color of the wall coverings.

- Use borders and edging to give a higher quality finish to fabric wall coverings.

Don't

- Put fabric in spaces which get dirty easily, like children's rooms or the kitchen.

- Abuse fabrics with striking decorative motifs or match fabrics with different patterns.

Tiles

The variety of tiles on the market opens an infinite world of decorative possibilities. Like with floor tiles, tiles for walls can be of different types, although they are less thick. If we consider the importance of taking great care when laying floors, it is even more so for the walls, as they are more visible. Tiles have traditionally been used in kitchens and bathrooms due to their resistance to water and the ease with which they are cleaned. These characteristics could be useful in other types of spaces, in which case we should not be shy of using them since they are among the most durable wall coverings. We should avoid abusing them since they can make a space seem too cold. In any case, consider the possibility of combining them with other materials such as paint or stucco.

Tiles, with their diverse finishes, offers us a whole world of combinations allowing functional spaces such as bathrooms or kitchens to also have aesthetical qualities.

The use of tiles is especially appropriate in spaces that must tolerate dampness and those which are constantly being cleaned like the kitchen or the bathroom.

Stucco

The application of traditional techniques such as stucco was lost with the introduction of more modern and less costly techniques, which do no require especially qualified professionals. The desire for an old-fashioned, handcrafted appearance has lead to some of these techniques being recovered, such as baked stucco, as well as giving rise to a growing number of techniques (most of which are paint-based), which attempt to imitate them.

If we are thinking of applying stucco we should bear in mind that baked stucco, following the traditional method, gives a glossy, resistant finish whose quality is superior to most other techniques. Obviously the cost is higher. Modern technology has made chemical products available, which have a similar appearance to stucco and similar benefits to stucco. In this case the choice of one method or the other will, without doubt, determine the cost.

Do

- Use stucco in frequently used spaces or even in the bathroom since they are highly resistant and washable.

- Use tiles in bathrooms and kitchens since they are water resistant and easily cleaned.

Don't

- Use porous tiles like terracotta in spaces such as the bathroom or the kitchen without giving them a special treatment to waterproof them.

- Use small tiles to cover large walls or large tiles for small walls.

Top 10 Tips

1 If you want to change the appearance of a room quickly and without too much expense, paint and paper together with fabrics will be your best allies.

2 The color of the walls can delineate different areas within the same space.

3 Baked stucco is impermeable and highly resistant, making it ideal for passageways or those that get dirty easily. It is also very warm and gives a high quality decorative finish.

4 Tiles are an ideal surface for bathrooms and kitchens. The large amount of models and finishes on the market opens up a world of decorative possibilities to us.

5 Be bold and use wood as a wall covering in spaces where traditionally it has not been used, such as the bathroom or the kitchen, always remembering to treat it appropriately against damp.

6 Marble is an ideal wall covering to create classical spaces, although it is also frequently used in more purist contemporary designs.

7 Natural fibers can be used as a wall covering, and are especially ideal for improving the acoustic conditions of a space.

8 Metal sheets or concrete are new materials, which are still not used very often. Try them out in passing spaces like passageways or hallways.

9 The stairs is an ideal place to experiment with different materials like iron or glass.

10 When choosing wall coverings bear in mind that they must match the floor, furniture... When choosing materials always bear in mind that the unity of the space must take priority.

Colors

Color is one of the most powerful tools in decoration. The predominant tone of a space will determine its character and atmosphere, which is why we need to recognize the possibilities and psychological effects of colors and the best ways to combine them.

Like artists, we all have our own palette. Over time and thanks to our personal development our palette changes, and this is reflected in the way we dress, the objects we possess and the decoration that surrounds us. By following some basic and simple guidelines we can bring more order and coherence to our palette and take full advantage of all the possibilities that color offers us.

Decoration must satisfy different needs, and among them the most notable are those that are personal, practical and social; color fulfills all three. Art and nature are the two most important sources of inspiration in decoration. The safest guide to follow when composing the colors that decorate a space is a picture or a scene that we see as being chromatically balanced and which reflects our color tastes. In the case of a picture, for example, we can analyze the importance and quantity of each of the colors on the canvas. We will also have to bear in mind the way in which these colors are distributed and how they relate with each other. Then we can try to reproduce this composition in our decoration, reproducing the same proportions and balance between the colors. Many other visual elements can be of use to us as a guide; an autumn scene with its light shades, a rug or a pattern....

The choice of color can make a room stimulating, balanced or practical. We need to organize the colors so that each space adopts the most appropriate character for the activities that will take place there. In a study we can create a stimulating space, while in the lounge a more relaxing character will dominate. Each color has its own personality, and whether we're looking for warmth, coldness, intimacy or serenity, we will always find a palette to satisfy our needs.

White and neutral colors

Yellows

Reds

Blues

Greens

Black

White and neutral colors

The color white, forever associated with pureness, is one of the most frequently used colors in decoration, due to how easily it combines with all tones. Neutral colors are those which contain a large amount of white in their composition, but whose tone has none of the primary or secondary colors. Pastel versions such as pale pink, or sky blue, therefore, are not included as neutral colors. Tones like cream or off-white, on the other hand, are considered to be neutral. We could say that the term neutral includes all the achromatic colors, although that would not be entirely true, since it includes tones like beige, which forms part of the family of browns, or the light grays, which in a way come from black.

Many neutral tones are connected with colors from nature: stone, earth, wood, esparto, sand, although they also come from artificial origin: metal, glass or concrete.

Neutral tones are especially practical in the world of decoration. The quality of neutral colors makes them easily combinable with other colors, and they do not lose their beauty over time. They are also gentle, calm and serene colors. Neutral colors, on the other hand, provide an appropriate background for displaying pictures and tapestries, and are ideal for decorating excessively loaded spaces or for making two different decoration styles sit well together, such as old architecture with modern furniture. Neutral tones are ideal for painting furniture, objects, walls or doors that we want to go unnoticed, or to remain in the background.

Another characteristic of neutral colors is that they provide a world of textures, as we have seen in a piece of furniture striped of this tone or in the multitude of neutral fabrics on the market, such as silks and tulles or sackcloth.

Traditional white used in lime or tempered form, had a texture that gave it a special effect, something which we do not find in the plastic paints more frequently used on the market. If we use this color in the traditional way, we will obtain a texture that creates a simple and rustic style.

White transmits serenity and relaxation to the spaces it decorates, and makes them appear larger and lighter, this is why it is especially appropriate for interior, dark or small rooms. Pure white, when hit by natural light, is a warm color, although under artificial light it can appear as a cold color. This is solved by adding a little pigment, which will give it a warm tone, whether it be red, yellowish or brown, and will maintain the property's of the white while affording it warmth.

In order for spaces to maintain the serenity that white provides, we must fill them with objects whose tones stay within the neutral range or at least close to it, or with natural textures using wood or stone. The confrontation of a picture with vivid colors, a vase of flowers or furniture with touches of gold with a neutral background will create an elegant contrast, and in a way, a sumptuous one.

Do	• Make the most of the tones' capacity for combining with difficult colors that do not accept other tones. • Introduce touches of color in the spaces where there are abundant neutral tones, otherwise they may appear boring. • Paint a small and interior room with neutral colors so that it appears larger and warmer, as well as lighter.	**Don't**	• Use bright or dark colors in rooms that are supposed convey tranquility. Neutral colors are more appropriate these cases. • Use neutral tones that lean towards blue or gray in co spaces, as they will not provide the warmth of yellowish reddish neutrals. • Use warm neutral tones in small spaces. The blue and gr variants will give spaces a greater sense of size.

Top 10 Tips

1 White and neutral colors give us the ideal background for a picture or tapestry to stand out on a wall.

2 In spaces loaded with architecture, and when we do not want the color to stand out, apply a neutral tone so that it remains in the background.

3 Neutral tones age well, so they can be used in places we do not paint often or which we want to look old.

4 The neutral variants are ideal for small spaces with little light.

5 White and the neutral tones are appropriate for combining different decorative styles, as they act as a neutral background of transition between one style and the other.

6 Neutral tones like metallic gray or concrete gray are especially advisable for creating modern spaces with aesthetics of technology.

7 The more textured tones, like lime or temper, are perfect for creating spaces with a slightly rustic aesthetic.

8 Fabrics with neutral colors, whether they be carpets, curtains or upholstery, are ideal for decoration because they go well with all other colors.

9 If we want a space with an abundance of neutral colors to appear more cheerful, we can introduce touches of colors that clash; the best colors for this are darker ones or even black.

10 A neutral tone is perfect for painting a wall, and the doors in that wall, which we want to go unnoticed.

Yellows

Yellow, the color of the sun, has historically only decorated the walls in the kitchen. This tendency has since been abandoned and now yellow is flooding all the rooms of the house, transmitting warmth and cheer. Yellow, like the light from the sun, is capable of cheering up the day for us, making it especially appropriate for a bedroom. The master impressionist Monet had his dining room decorated with yellow tones, which gave it an exceptional warmth. Yellow, whether in its lighter versions or through the yellowish light provided by an incandescent light, floods spaces, creating exceptionally cozy atmospheres. Its association with the sun has lead it to be used more in tropical and Mediterranean countries, above all in coastal areas, due to its association with the summer and heat.

It is a color that is difficult to handle because it easily stands out and draws a lot of attention. This is why its use has extended into commercial environments and as a symbol of attention, which unfor-tunately has damaged its reputation in the world of decoration. Due to its capacity to draw attention we must take care not to use it disproportionately. It has been psychologically proved that a small amount is enough to give people a beneficial effect. Yellow can be useful for converting white into a creamy color or a very light yellow that lends a room warmth, which can not be obtained by using white. Yellow is not always a warm color: it is the red that provides this warmth. A pure, citric yellow can, therefore, be a cold color.

Throughout history yellow has been connected with certain negative aspects. It is said, for example, to bring bad luck to actors who wear it on stage, and is also considered the color of madness. In the history of art there is a key representative of yellow in painting: Vincent van Gogh. His well-known paintings of sunflowers and fields of corn offer us an example of the multitude of shades of yellow available to us, and of the warmth and expression they afford.

White and yellow are easily com-bined. White helps to accentuate the warmth of yellow, as well as calming its vividness.

Yellow transmits energy and warmth;
it is ideal for making spaces such as
a kitchen or a bedroom seem cozier.

<table>
<tr><td>Do</td><td><ul><li>Apply yellow to white to accentuate its warmth.</li><li>Combine it with greens, blues and vivid pinks.</li><li>Apply it in dark and cold rooms to bring warmth and enhance any natural light.</li></ul></td></tr>
</table>

Do

- Apply yellow to white to accentuate its warmth.

- Combine it with greens, blues and vivid pinks.

- Apply it in dark and cold rooms to bring warmth and enhance any natural light.

Don't

- Combine it with pastel tones, since these seem sad alongside yellow.

- Use a very intense yellow as it could stand out too much and require equally energetic colors to complement it.

- Abuse the golden shades of yellow, although they give a lot of warmth when used in moderation, they can make spaces seem too ostentatious and cold if they are abused.

The yellow family

We can group yellows used in decoration into four large families.

Citric yellows, which are bright and luminous, create a cheerful atmosphere full of energy and add a flavor of youthfulness. Some of its variants strongly catch our attention. We should avoid using extremely citric tones, as they can seem too acidic.

Ochres and natural yellows, which also bring light but are duller, offer a warm atmosphere, less cheerful and energetic, but clean, ordered and to a certain degree sumptuous. These are variants, which are fairly common in nature and give a space a natural air.

The egg yolk yellows contain red in their composition, which gives them even more warmth and energy. They are very vivid tones that have a powerful presence, which is why they should be combined with equally vivid tones. They are difficult to use in large quantities, but are ideal for accentuating other tones or as details and touches of color combined with patterns and wallpaper. Orange with a high red content lends a space a very warm, tropical air.

Golden yellows, copper and tin offer quality, opulence, class and even luxury to the places they decorate. They must be used with care and shouldn't be abused. Avoid creating spaces that lose quality because they appear too luxurious.

Yellow tones combine especial well with natural colors such as th of wood.

Top 10 Tips

1 Yellow has positive connotations due to its association with sunlight and warm countries.

2 Being a warm color, it produces the sensation that objects of this color (and of other warm colors) are closer.

3 Yellow, due to its warmth and association with natural light, is ideal for dark and cold rooms.

4 The paler variant is very versatile and combines with gray, cool blue and lavender, making them more cheerful.

5 It is the ideal color for converting an excessively sumptuous passageway into a homely space.

6 The combination of yellow and violet produces a vibrant and exciting contrast, which is appropriate for rooms with lots of activity.

7 Intense yellow can be very warm but needs to be combined with tones of equal intensity and energy, which may make a room seem too striking.

8 To enhance the warmth of yellow tones we can combine them with white tones.

9 Yellow appears cheerful alongside colors like gray, cool blue or lavender.

10 The Golden and copper tones of yellow are perfect for creating elegant, sumptuous and classy spaces.

Reds

When we think of the color red, many associations come to mind. Red is the color of passion, fire, blood... and historically associated with danger, it is used throughout the world of communication as an effective way of getting attention. It is a dominant and provocative color, which we relate with movement.

Its use in decoration is concentrated mainly in the dining and lounge areas. This has a clear explanation: its psychological effects. From studies of the effects each color has on humans, it has been discovered that red is a color that stimulates the appetite and the desire for conversation, making it highly appropriate in these rooms. When used in large quantities, red causes discharges of adrenalin into the blood, accelerates the heartbeat and creates a sensation of heat. Although there are many shades of red in nature, such as the sky and sunset or terracotta, it is difficult to find much pure red. It does appear however, in small traces that decorate the landscape, such as for example the poppies dotted around a green meadow. Contrary to this, in the world of art there are numerous artists who have felt attracted by the energy red exudes in its purest state. Among these, outstanding figures like Mondrian, Calder, Miró or Lichtenstein, who combine basic colors in their purest forms with black and white.

Due to the intensity and energy that red exudes, we must use it with caution and avoid large surfaces of this color. In decoration the application of this color is more appropriate in city homes, since in the countryside or the mountains yellows, neutral tones or even greens and blues are more common. A bordeaux or an vermilion provides a sumptuousness, which can be appropriate for classical and serious rooms. In its pure state, red is appropriate for more radical combinations of colors and contrasts. Colors like crimson red may be too intense; it is more advisable in small details, which lend energy to the whole or to opt for less intense and striking colors. Let's consider the versions of red which are most abundant in nature. Red from terracotta or wood are highly appropriate tones for decoration and provide warmth as well as energy, without attracting too much attention. Clay is another good example of these tones that we should not hesitate to use. Scarlet, which is brighter, is ideal for decorating homely rooms like the dining room, the lounge and even a bedroom. This color offers an especially attractive result when seen by candlelight.

Red is a bold and energetic colo[r] without doubt the most ideal fo[r] introducing an element of contra[st] or a touch of color in an otherwis[e] monotonous space.

Do

- Use pink in spaces which are normally used at night, as under candlelight or soft lighting it can exude a very special warmth.

- Use pink in small and dark spaces since it provides light and a greater sense of size.

- Use more natural shades of red like earth or terracotta to decorate spaces we want to look both rustic and warm.

Don't

- Use very cold shades of pink (those that contain blue their composition) in cold and dark areas.

- Use versions of pink traditionally associated with feminin ity and those frequently used for decorating girls' be rooms.

- Use dark shades of red to decorate dimly lit space Although they provide warmth they will also make th room seem even darker.

The red family

Pure red is the brightest and most luminous shade of red and suggests movement, warmth and passion.

We should try not to abuse these variants, since they ought to be combined with tones of a similar magnitude, and may give rise to spaces with great chromatic intensity that are somewhat tiring on the eyes.

Vermilion or **bordeaux** is less bright but equally intense. It transmits elegance, sumptuousness and opulence to the spaces it decorates. Its earthy tones give it a rustic, autumnal and warming air, which we can complement with

blues, greens, whites and even gold.

The **versions of pink** deserve a special mention since they are quite different to the reds. It is a friendly, luxurious and pleasant color, which when used in its different shades lends warmth and energy to spaces without attracting too much attention, as the reds do. Pay special attention to the choice of pink and avoid those that have been used historically to identify femininity or to decorate little girls' bedrooms. Shades of pink combine well with white and variants of blue, and form a harmonious contrast with yellows.

Top 10 Tips

1 In dimly lit rooms pinks, which belong to the warmer section on the color wheel, allow us to introduce warm and dynamic contrasts.

2 An intense red gives a vibrant and energetic sensation making it ideal for decorating spaces like the dining room or lounge.

3 A carpet with shades of red is a decorative object par excellence, as it offers a space warmth and color.

4 Paint objects we want to become a point of visual attraction in red.

5 Darker versions of red, like bordeaux, are ideal to combine with golden tones and to create sumptuous and elegant spaces.

6 Red is a frequently used color in modern and high-tech fashions, as it fills atmospheres with energy and movement.

7 It is intensely striking. We should not use it in large quantities because, very often, it is enough in touches.

8 Natural reds, contrary to the intense red, go unnoticed and are especially appropriate for spaces with a rustic atmosphere.

9 The combination of red and green, its complement, produces a vibrant effect, which works especially well in spaces of activity like the dining room.

10 Pink is a color that offers us many possibilities in the world of decorations. Less bold than red, but equally warm and easier to combine with.

Blues

The blue of the sky, the blue of the sea... The different variants of blue bathe natural spaces in their beauty. Blue is the color found most abundantly in nature, and its tone range, is definitely the most extensive. Because of its relation with large natural spaces, blue transmits peace, tranquility and freedom, freshness and cleanliness. Furthermore, blue tones combine with all colors, so we could consider it to be the most neutral of all the primary colors. Its association with the sea affords it depth, and its relation with the sky, nobility.

Blue can work well in any room of the house. In the bedroom it is said to enhance our capacity to remember dreams; it will make a living room feel airy, spacious and tranquil. It is ideal for the bathroom, where it gives a feeling of cleanliness and evokes water. These characteristics make it equally appropriate in the kitchen, whether on tiles or decorative objects such as crockery, jugs, etcetera.

We must exercise caution when choosing blue to decorate spaces. Pure blues from the middle of the color range may seem cold, but this sensation can be avoided by using those that incorporate reds, oranges or yellows, or which lean towards violet or green. A badly chosen blue can make a dark space with little sunlight appear cold.

Blue is an easy color for the human eye to assimilate, making it a calm and pleasant color. In its stronger versions, with touches of cobalt and ultramarine, blue acquires a sumptuous and elegant air, which is ideal for classical spaces. Indigo is also appropriate in these cases. By combining different shades of blue, we could obtain a space that appears to cold; therefore, we should opt to combine it with other colors, taking advantage of its versatility.

Blue has been a highly valued color throughout the history of art. The use of the lapis lazuli by the Egyptians is a good example of this. Among modern artists who have worked wonders with blue we must mention Vassily Kandinsky, who combines shades of blue in such a way that this color acquires an intense power of expression. Also Pablo Picasso, who in his famous blue period, showed us the endless different variations we can achieve with a single color, turning it into a tool for expression.

Blue provides tranquility and relaxation; it is perfect for decorating recreational spaces like the lounge, especially if this is in contact with nature.

Do

- Use blue to make spaces or objects in this color appear further away or so that they lose importance and move out of the foreground.

- The more neutral, pale and discrete shades of blue are ideal for creating neutral and relaxing atmospheres.

- In spaces where blue seems too cold, we can introduce warmth through yellow and orange.

Don't

- The grayish versions of blue can seem excessively sad; should avoid combining them with cold colors. We c make them more cheerful by combining them with wa or neutral shades.

- Combine blue with red, cyan with orange and gray-b with yellowish red, as they may produce a vibrant and p sibly bothersome effect on the decoration, assuming thi not the effect we are looking for.

- Decorate interior bedrooms in blue or those without na ral light, because although they will appear larger, t will also seem colder.

The blue family

Sky blue and pastel tones of blue bring light and depth to rooms, making them especially appropriate in small spaces. This range also includes tones that contain red in their composition, which gives them a higher level of quality and makes them ideal for dark and cold spaces. They are refreshing and discrete tones, which are easy to combine and adapt to many spaces.

The range of blues, **turquoise** and **aquamarine** has in its composition a high content of green, allowing it to combine easily with all greens and their derivatives, as well as the colors found between orange and red, complements of blue and green respectively. They also combine with shades of violet and yellow to create fresh and fun spaces. Turquoise brings serenity and freshness to a room, and works well in combination with natural materials like wood or plants.

Lavender with its shades of pink, falls into the warm variants of blue, and is ideal for rustic and calm spaces.

The versions of **blue indigo** and **ultramarine** are more intense and possess more personality; they are, therefore ideal for spaces like the dining room or the lounge. If we add white to their composition, we will obtain colors which are less strong and easier to use and combine. Being intense tones, when we combine them we should do so with colors of equal intensity or attempt to calm them down by introducing white into their composition.

The **grayish blues** work especially well for highly elegant decorations.

Top 10 Tips

1 To bring more harmony to spaces we can combine blue with other colors of a similar intensity, for example sky blue with pale green.

2 If we want to create fun contrasts, we can join blue with complementary tones: terracotta or yellows and oranges.

3 Blue diffuses and softens intense sunlight, and can, therefore, calm bedrooms which are flooded with light.

4 It is a color, which, due to its relaxing qualities, is ideal for places that require tranquility and concentration, like areas of study.

5 For a room to appear larger we can decorate it with light and cold tones like sky blue.

6 To decorate small rooms and those without natural light, we should use the warmer versions like violet, as the purer or grayish shades seem too cold without natural light.

7 We can use blue in bathrooms because of its capacity to express cleanliness and evoke water, although we should introduce warm touches so it does not appear too cold.

8 In the kitchen, blue is always welcome, whether for tiles or for the crockery, and it goes well with stainless steel, which is being used more and more.

9 Blue combined with white produces a seaside and fresh sensation and if we also add a little red we obtain a sporty effect, ideal for homes by the beach or to decorate bedrooms with motifs related to the sea.

10 The darker shades of blue, such as navy or cobalt are ideal for creating sumptuous spaces.

Greens

Just by going to the garden or out into the woods we discover the infinite range of greens that nature showers us with. Leaves, stalks, moss, grass...each of which shows off a different shade, but there is harmony between all of them. The example of nature, which combines greens with majestic elegance, is proof that this is one of the colors that allows for most combinations between its different shades. In the same way as observing a picture helps us to create a balanced color scheme, observing the greens that the landscape is composed of or those combined in a plant or a group of plants will give us inspira-tion for spaces using green. Green, therefore, allows us —unlike with other colors— to create a room using a single basic color, by com-bining its different variants.

The dominant shades of green that we choose for a spaces depends on how we are going to use it. Bright greens are intrinsically youthful and fresh; the darker ver-sions like olive or moss are more serious and mature.

As we can observe in nature, greens combine very well with reds and pinks. We can also obtain a good combination with different tones of its complement, blue, such as the pastels and turquoise.

- Take advantage of green's properties to connect exterior and interior areas of the home.

- Combine it with its complementary color, red, creating a sensation of movement and a vibrant effect.

- Draw on nature, combining it with pinks, yellows, reds and even shades of green.

- Paint objects or walls we want to stand out in green, this is a neutral tone that sends objects into the bac ground.

- Abuse greens combining many of their versions in a sing space. Green by itself is a color that can appear boring a too neutral.

- Combine green with shades of lilac or magenta, becau although this will produce an interesting contrast, it m be irritating when used in decoration.

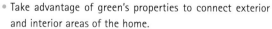

The green family

The lighter shades of green, like **sage** or **pistachio**, with a high content of white, combine with neutral colors, pale pink and gold. When these shades incorporate yellow in their composition they provide light and warmth to dark rooms.

More citric shades of green, like **lime green**, combine well with each other and give spaces vitality. They can be combined with yellows, accompanied by blues or reds, but the earthy shades will give them more power.

Pure green, like **apple green**, is a Mediterranean and warm variant that combines with intense blue or yellow, creating areas that evoke the Caribbean and coastal places. These shades are appropriate especially in spaces with rustic furnishings. It is, therefore, a cheerful and lively color that affords warmth to spaces.

The stronger shades of green, like **emerald green** or **bottle green**, combine with intense and sometimes dark versions of red, orange and yellow. Nature is a good example of these combinations of green with the colors most commonly found in flowers. When used in rooms with little light we can combine them with white, which will transmit luminosity to the spaces.

The **grayish greens** or those that lean towards brown must be used with care, because they can darken interior and cold spaces, and ideally should be combined with natural materials with brown or reddish shades, such as wood or terracotta. For furniture, these shades combine very well with light, modern pieces. If we want to give an informal flavor to spaces where these variants are dominant, we can incorporate a creamy color.

Top 10 Tips

1 Nature offers us endless combinations of green that we can use as models to create decorative schemes.

2 The more intense and brighter greens give spaces a youthful ambiance; darker greens, on the other hand, are more mature.

3 Green is the ideal color to create a symbolic join between an interior space and an exterior one, especially places directly connected with a garden.

4 Green, as nature has shown us, combines very well with the colors of flowers, like yellow, red, pink... If we apply these combinations to decoration, we will obtain a fresh and natural space.

5 The medium and dark shades of green, like olive and moss, are the best for rustic spaces, because they combine well with browns, earthy colors and neutral colors that are often dominant in these types of decorations.

6 The more intense and luminous versions of green, like lime or pistachio, are reminiscent of Caribbean or Mediterranean places, and so transmit a sensation of warmth and fun.

7 Because of its association with nature and freshness, green is ideal for creating tranquil and serene spaces.

8 Green, in some of its shades, is fairly neutral, making it an easy color to use with other shades.

9 The lighter and softer tones of green create simple and tranquil spaces, which always feel homely.

10 The combination of green with some of the variants of blue, such as turquoise or the pastels, is ideal for creating spaces that require concentration and tranquility.

Black

A possible way to divide the chromatic circle is by separating the warm colors from the cold. Black is produced when a body absorbs all light waves without reflecting any. It is exceedingly apt for creating contrast, since together with other shades, particularly warm ones, it achieves highly expressive combinations. Black is not an appropriate color, however, for dominating large proportions of a decorative scheme.

Decorating with black requires very clear planning beforehand. If you are not used to working or dealing with this color in any way, it requires a certain predisposition, as it is difficult to imagine the final effect. We must pay special attention as if mistakes are made, they are difficult to correct, various layers are needed of a light base before we can start working with a newly chosen color and totally counteract the effect.

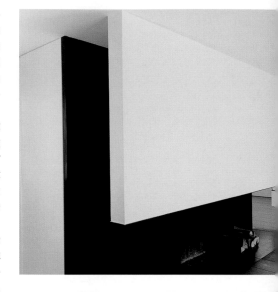

However, both black and dark colors in general, can be striking in the appropriate environment, with abundant natural light or a well positioned artificial light, as long as they are combined with complementary tones.

In large spaces it is very useful, as it offers the possibility of enhancing certain areas and offers greater depth. On the other hand, it is not at all advisable in small rooms with little light, like hallways, where we could feel suffocated.

Certain shapes of a room can be enhanced by juxtapositioning black and other lighter tones. Rugs, curtains and furniture in general play, in these cases, an important role in avoiding an excessively somber atmosphere.

Black contrasts well with white, yellow and the lighter colors, making it ideal for achieving bold and striking effects.

Black is ideal as a contrasting element that breaks with the monotony of the rest of a space.

- Use black to create contrasting elements in spaces that appear monotonous.

- Combine black with lighter colors like white, yellow and shades of gray.

- Always apply black in moderation and in small quantities to avoid dark and somber spaces.

- Combine black with other dark tones like browns, da greens or navy blue.

- Use black in small spaces and those without natural lig like hallways and passageways.

- Put large amounts of black in small spaces, even if they a well lit. Black is a color that we must apply in moderatic

Top 10 Tips

1 Black is ideal for introducing a contrast into a monotonous space.

2 Paint objects black if we want them to stand out or contrast with everything else.

3 Avoid applying large stretches of black, as it will make spaces seem dark.

4 Black combined with shades of gray create serious but extremely elegant spaces.

5 Use black in large spaces to enhance certain elements or bring greater depth.

6 Avoid using black in small spaces or those that receive little natural light.

7 If we want to produce contrasts, use black together with light colors like white or yellow.

8 Black does not go well with dark colors like browns, greens or dark blues.

9 The decision to apply black must be well thought out and carefully studied since replacing it afterwards can be somewhat costly.

10 In small, well-lit spaces we can use black in moderation, but only in small quantities.

Lighting a space

The first and most basic consideration to bear in mind when planning the lighting of a space is the capacity and state of the wiring. Secondly we have to consider the needs of each of the spaces, which will be determined by the activities that will take place within them. Although the lounge is a recreational space, which does not require a specific type of lighting, let's consider, for example, that this room may, on occasion, be used as a work place, like a study or an area for reading, and will therefore need lighting appropriate to these activities. After establishing what our lighting needs for the space, we need to decide what will be the focal points of the room. An old piece of furniture or some pictures on a wall could become the focus of attention if we use the right lighting. In spaces that are spread out and not particularly unitary it may be of interest to enhance the idea of a whole, and it will, therefore, be more important to increase the ambient lighting.

On the market we can find different types of light sources, each of which produces different lighting and a different color. When choosing one light or another we should find out what tone the light produces to then see if it will adapt to

the colors of the room it will be used in. We must also be aware that each color may be appropriate for a particular activity. White light, for example, is not very appropriate for reading or writing as it makes the paper seem so white that it may irritate our eyes. In this case we could choose a blue bulb, which calms the white of the paper as well as transmitting a sensation of relaxation.

Another important aspect to take into consideration when planning the lighting of a space is that it must be versatile enough to adapt to the changing needs of each of the spaces in the house. A bedroom could, for example, be a place for relaxation, requiring soft lighting, although it could also be a place for work, requiring a specific lighting that adapts to the needs of the activities that take place there. We need to distinguish between the different types of lighting:

Ambient lighting is that of the background, it provides a general light, which is uniform and lends balance and unity to a space. This type of light is often achieved via indirect lights such as ceiling or wall lamps.

Task lighting is that which offers the amount of light necessary to carry out specific tasks like eating,

reading, preparing food... and it is achieved using more or less specific light sources, such as a halogen bulb, fluorescent lighting or a table or foot lamp.

Decorative lighting is that which has an aesthetic function rather than a practical one, such as enhancing a particular piece of furniture, a picture or an architectural feature using a wide variety of light sources such as spotlights or picture lights. In this sense we must also consider light sources as decorative features in themselves; for example candles, which are more often used for their aesthetical value than their functional one.

Lamps are also a decorative object, so we should not only examine the light they produce, but also consider that they have to adapt to the style of the room where they are located.

When planning the lighting of a space, we must not only consider the large quantity of lights the market has to offer us, but also the varying switches that allow us to regulate the quantity of light, thereby being easily adapted to our needs. At all times we must consider that the more flexible the lighting the better it can be adapted to suit out needs and, therefore, be more functional and comfortable. The flexibility of a lighting scheme is

also based on the possibility to light, independently, the different elements, and be able to use them in different combinations.

The efficiency of good lighting is related to the correct positioning of the light switches, which allow us to control the different light sources and avoid the use of extension leads. As a general rule, we should position a switch at the entrance of each of the rooms and close to the bed, sofa or the place where we are going to be for most of the time, for example, the desk in an office. Also we should put at least one switch on each of the walls, although if the wall is very long we can spread them out along it every so many meters or according to the needs dictated by the furniture or other decorative features. In spaces like the kitchen or the bathroom, where we have to plug in appliances, we must ensure that the plug sockets are as far as possible from water, on top of worktops and behind appliances like the fridge or dishwasher. Another aspect to consider when planning is the presence of children or people with special requirements. In the case of children we should avoid using foot or table lamps and consider the height of the lamps to avoid a glare.

Types of light sources

The different light sources on the market adapt to each of the needs of the different activities we may carry out at home.

Light fixtures are different supports for the bulbs, which, in turn, may be different shapes and give a wide variety of different types of light. Light bulbs, through a phenomena know as incandescence, produce light, which is projected and diffused by one way or another depending on the design of the lamp and the shade, if there is one.

Today's designers are showing great interest in researching the possibilities of light, which has lead to the creation of new models of lamps that offer a wide range of possibilities to meet our needs.

The design of the fixture or the shade determines the way in which the light is projected. Shades that give off light without a beam are called diffusers, and those that direct the light are known as projectors. Diffusers may be on the wall, ceiling, tabletop or on a foot lamp.

Types of electric light sources

Light parameters

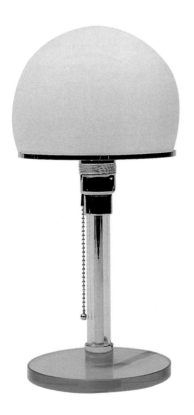

Types of electric light sources

There are two large groups of lights, according to the light production system: incandescent lights and discharge lights.

Incandescent lights are those that produce light using an electric current that comes through a tungsten wire, which heats up from the electricity until it becomes incandescent and produces luminous energy. An example of this type of light is the classical and well-known light bulb, which gives off a yellowish, warm light. These types of light sources are also known as tungsten lights. Incandescent lights have different forms, such as projectors or tubes, which are not used very often in homes.

Discharge lights are based on luminescence, which is produced when a discharge of electricity is generated in a gaseous atmosphere. The best known are fluorescent and neon, both of which are tubular.

They also have the shape of an ampoule, but in these the luminescence comes from a mercury vapor. The light produced by this type of source differs from that of the incandescent lights basically because it is whiter or more blue and colder −incandescent bulbs give off heat, but the discharge ones do not−. Despite this basic difference we must remember that both types of light have a multitude of variants that offer very different types of light, which will almost definitely adapt to our needs.

ight parameters

he research on the physical parameters of light helps us derstand how light acts on different elements and how its qualies can be useful when it comes to coration.

e intensity of light should be derstood as the amount of light hitted.

hen overwhelmingly bright, hether the source is natural or tificial, light is commonly deribed as intense. The dazzle is oduced when an excessive mount of light reaches our eyes, when a strong contrast occurs tween a brightly illuminated zone d a dimly illuminated zone. These uations should be avoided. Qual- of light does not correlate with e number of light fixtures. The wrong type of lighting can wear out our vision, so monotonous and dimly lit rooms should be avoided as much as strong light contrasts and excessively illuminated rooms. Reflection happens when a ray of light touches a surface, which, in turn, returns a part of this light. There are two types of reflection depending on the surfaces:

Specular or directed reflection takes place when the rays of light are projected onto a shiny surface, such as a mirror or something silver, for example. The effect is a dazzling shine caused by a large number of the rays being reflected in the same direction. Due to the negative effects the glare causes, where possible, we should avoid these types of reflections.

Diffused reflection occurs when the surface the light is projected onto is matt, such as a brick or painted wall, for example. In this case the rays are projected in all directions, making the light diffuse throughout the space. The degree of reflection is determined by the color of the surface. Darker colors reflect less light that lighter ones, which is why dark rooms should be painted in the latter. White, for example, reflects around 80-90% of the light that it receives, while colors like dark green reflect only around 20%.

The reflection can light up a space by what is called indirect lighting. This type of lighting is based on the light projected by the surfaces. Consider for example, the light that a white wall would reflect if we used spotlights to cast light onto it. The space would be lit by the light reflected in the wall, and so the ambient lighting of the space would be that produced by the phenomenen of reflection. Indirect lighting is not appropriate for task lighting, so we will always use it to provide ambient lighting.

Table lamps

This name encompasses those light sources that have been designed to go on top of a more or less high surface, so they often have a base or a pincer. The function and aesthetics of this type of light is very varied and depends on the light source, the shade or diffuser and its strength. These lights often produce a focused, localized light, in order to create focal points or light up certain areas of a room. A table light is a good instrument for task lighting needed for a particular activity, such as reading or sewing. In this case we should be careful where we put the light in relation to ourselves, since they can produce shadows, which may irritate. If the function of the light is purely aesthetical then the choice of color for the shade will be determined by aesthetical criteria only. If the aim is functional, we should choose a color for the shade that filters the light in a tone appropriate to the activity we are going to carry out, as some colors may tire the eyes. Table lamps are ideal as extra lighting and to make up for deficient ambient lighting.

Foot lamps

Foot lamps are those that support themselves and do not require any supporting elements, whether horizontal or vertical. This is why foot lamps are a decorative element in themselves. The great advantage of this type of light is that they are independent and so can be moved. This implies versatility and adaptability to spaces with changing needs, such as the living room.

The wide variety of foot lamps on the market makes it impossible to define the type of light they give off. Some produce a light similar to that of table lamps, while others cast light towards the ceiling or floor or create ambient lighting; we will almost undoubtedly find a foot lamp that suits our needs. Like table lamps they can have an auxiliary function making them ideal for decorating a reading corner or lighting an insufficiently lit dining room... Generally these lights are adjustable in height and offer the possibility of being set in different positions, making them even more versatile and practical. Some lights are also sold with a dimmer switch incorporated, so we can graduate the light intensity depending on our needs, without having to install a switch especially for this purpose.

Hanging or ceiling lamps

anging lamps, often used traditionally, offer a general light, which is often insufficient. In buildings with high ceilings this insufficiency is even more accentuated. We can use this type of light, therefore, to achieve global lighting, which lends unity to a space, but we must always bear in mind that this type of light will not be sufficient for specific activities. The use of a large or wide shade will allow the light to spread generously throughout a space, and we should always avoid using shades that project a clear dividing line on the wall between a lit area and a dark one. When positioning this type of light it is very important to calculate the ideal height, thus avoiding the light impeding the vision between the different diners. An ideal solution to this problem are hanging lamps with adjustable heights, which are very comfortable and versatile.

Hanging lamps are ideal for lighting up tables such as the dining table, creating around them a homely center of reunion, defined by the light. With large spaces, like a living room-diner, this type of light is very useful to differentiate the different zones if we position it above the table and light the rest of the room with other types of lights.

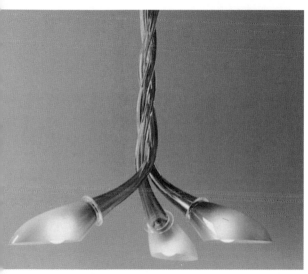

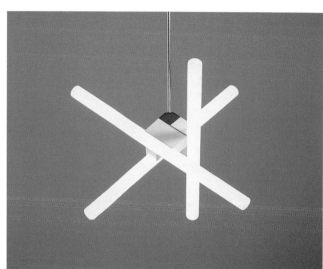

Flush-mount lights

Used very regularly in decoration today, flush-mount lights are composed of a body, which is hidden in the ceiling and casts a light downwards. There is a multitude of different models, but broadly speaking, among the most common types are lights directed downwards, adjustable flush-mount spotlights and standard spotlights. Some are not entirely flush-mount and are complemented by an exterior fixture that controls the lights either by diffusing it like a shade or directing it. This type of lighting is often used in groups of lights distributed around the ceiling, which are controlled using one or several switches, although normally a single switch dominates several points of light.

To obtain efficient lighting in large spaces it is advisable to distribute the control of the different lights across different switches providing the lighting with a certain amount of flexibility. When dealing with fixed lights we must carefully study and calculate their position to ensure they suit our needs. Fixed lighting is often used as an ambient lighting, although if this is not the case and we want it to be for task, we should consider even more carefully what the best layout will be. If it will be used as ambient lighting, then the different support lights like foot or table lamps will help us to adapt the lighting to different situations. In a lounge, for example, if we only use flush-mount lights, we will obtain a cold and not particularly comfortable lighting; it is advisable then to complement it with task lighting.

Adjustable flush-mount lights allow fixed lighting to adapt, to a certain degree, to the changing situations of a modern house. Other flush-mount lights such as those that are height-adjustable allow for a certain amount of flexibility that can also be useful. Changing the shade, the bulb and even the lens can convert a fixed light into one that can change depending on the desired atmosphere or our needs.

We should also include in this section flush-mount lights that are concealed in architectural features like cornices and ceilings. This type of lighting is purely decorative and is perfect for making a cold and empty space into something more interesting and warmer.

Flush-mount lights can be almost unnoticeable elements, and so ideal for spaces where we want lighting to be adequate but not obvious.

Track lighting

This system of lighting is formed by two basic elements: a track that acts as support and a series of light sources attached to this in such a way as to allow their mobility. The main feature of this type of lighting is, therefore, versatility. Although tracks are often no longer than two or three feet, track lighting is often used to light large spaces. Furthermore, they are modular, so several tracks can be connected to form a single longer one, or even a square structure of tracks.

The versatility of this system is partly based on the possibility of moving the different lights along the track, as the electricity either arrives to them via wires hidden inside the track or through the actual track acting as a conductor of electricity. Also, the lights on this type of feature are, in most cases, adjustable, so the light can be focused where we want it to be. If we also consider the possibility of changing the light sources, we can introduce even more changes.

If we look at lighting in museums or art galleries, we will see that for the most part they use tracks: it is the only type of lighting that adapts to the different needs of these spaces. If we are thinking of lighting a space that will experience dramatic changes over time, for example, a children's room, or if we simple like to make frequent changes to the positions of furniture or pictures, track lighting may be very useful to us.

Spotlights

Spotlights can be used as part of a track or independently. In both cases there are different types: with standard bulbs, with big bulbs and an incorporated reflector or with halogen bulbs of different sizes, although the smaller ones are better as they produce a narrower beam of light, which is more appropriate for lighting specific objects.

In terms of how to use spotlights, there are different types of lighting for different purposes. If we cast the lights downwards we will achieve a specific light on the objects beneath and cast shadows onto the floor. We could change the angle slightly making somewhat bigger shadows but avoiding bothering reflections in horizontal surfaces.

By casting the light upwards we will achieve a very decorative and ambient lighting, since the light that is reflected downwards will not be enough to carry out any sort of specific activity. This is not a particularly common form of lighting because it requires the installation of the light points at a low level, thereby rendering them less practical. Today on the market, there are a number of foot lamps designed to light the ceiling, which is how this type of lighting is used most. By lighting the ceiling we give it greater importance or even make it the main feature; this is why it would be advisable if we have a ceiling of architectural value, such as an old ceiling decorated with a cornice and rosettes.

Spotlights directed at the walls make rooms seem bigger and play a decorative role by bathing the walls in light or lighting objects such as a picture or a tapestry. If we want the spotlights to carry out the latter role we should place them close to the wall, but if we just want them to light the wall, they should be positioned 2 or 3 feet away from the wall.

If we use spotlights to light up a workplace, ensure that the shadows they cast do not fall directly onto the work surface, as this could be bothersome.

Wall lamps

Wall lamps can be used for two different functions: to provide ambient or task lighting. It is very common to use wall lamps to give ambient lighting to a space such as a passageway or hallway, where, since they are passing areas, foot lamps do not seem appropriate. They are also used for lighting specific areas. Some wall lamps produce a light directed upwards and others cast light downwards, both can be adapted to different lighting needs. A wall lamp that casts light downwards, for example, would be ideal to light a picture or old piece of furniture. If the light is projected upwards it can be used in a similar way to the spotlights when directed upwards.

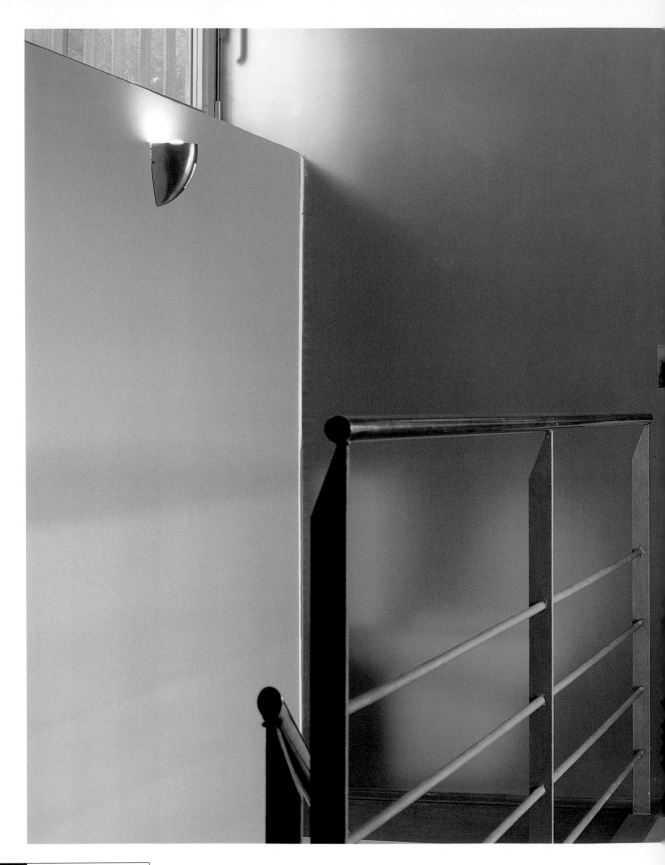

Top 10 Tips

1 Light colors reflect more light, making them ideal for dark spaces.

2 To calm down excessive lighting in a room we can use dark tones to absorb the light.

3 Also consider the difference between artificial light sources and natural ones like candles, a fireplace..., which have a high decorative value.

4 Ambient or general lighting will make a small space seem larger.

5 Task lighting will fragment the perception of a space making it appear smaller or dividing into sub-spaces.

6 The lighting of a space must allow for a multitude of variations so that it can be adapted to the changing needs of different situations.

7 It is important to consider the capacity and state of the existing installation before planning the new lighting.

8 When choosing an electrical source we should find out how much light it produces and what tone it acquires to be sure it will suit the room we are lighting.

9 Each activity has an appropriate light source; for example, a bluish light is ideal for reading and study.

10 When planning the lighting of a space we should consider the presence of children or people who may have special requirements.

Hallways and entrances

The entrance, which is often for-gotten, is a space of great importance in a home. We must remember that the hallway is the first room that a visitor will see and will, therefore, be their first impression of us. So we must consider that the entrance reflects our personality. If we want our house to seem warm to the visitor, we must decorate and light the entrance in a way that transmits this feeling. A combination of flush-mount lights or wall lamps with table or foot lamps will provide a warm and homely atmosphere for an appreciative visitor.

The entrance is the space in the house, which, due to its function, allows us to be most theatrical when planning its decoration and lighting. Spotlights that cast dramatic shadows or a foot lamp that gives off a special light are examples of elements that, in other spaces, would appear out of place, but in the entranceway offer pleasing results.

Passageways and stairs

Passageways are, in general, passing areas where no specific activity takes place, so there is no need for anything more than appropriate ambient lighting. On the other hand, we must also consider that they are often spaces between different rooms with different lighting. The human eye can adapt to changes in light but these changes should not be excessive. So we can use the passageway, for example, as a transitional space between the abundant light of a lounge to a dimly lit interior bathroom.

Stairways require special treatment as they are spaces where a practical and functional lighting is more important that a decorative one. In many cases, stairways do not have their own lighting, but depend on that of adjacent rooms; this, however, is something we should try to avoid. We must give these spaces their own, appropriate lighting using light sources that highlight the different vertical and horizontal planes that the stairs are composed of. On the landings we can use a less direct and more ambient lighting, such as wall lamps for example. Both in passageways and on the stairs, the positioning of the switches is almost as important as the lighting itself. Since these are passing spaces it must be practical and we must be able to operate the lights quickly. To achieve an effective distribution we should study which are the most common movements through the spaces.

Kitchens

Kitchens are work spaces that require abundant and practical lighting. Generous, ceiling lighting will be enough for ambient lighting, but insufficient for working with, and may cause bothersome shadows on the work area. The use of a hanging light may be appropriate for a kitchen's small dining area. The work areas, however, require task lighting through spotlights or fluorescent tubes, whether flush or visible. The spotlights must be positioned above or in front of the person who is working; if they are behind they will cause unwanted shadows. Fluorescent tubes are not attractive and are often hidden beneath the high furnishings of the kitchen, they do, however, offer adequate light for this room, as well as being more economical than the spotlights.

Bathrooms

The case of the bathroom is similar to that of the kitchen. We should use an abundant ambient lighting for which halogen bulbs are ideal, as they produce a clean and bright light. The sink and mirror area requires task lighting as this is the most important part of the bathroom. The most ideal lighting for the mirror is lateral lighting, like those found in dressing rooms, using several low-voltage bulbs; this avoids any shadows. In the bathroom we must be very careful not to position any plug sockets, light switches or light sources too close to water. If the circumstances make it impossible to avoid then we should consult a specialist who can give us advice about lighting systems that are appropriate for wet places.

In the bathroom, lights with halogen bulbs are often used as they give a bluish light, which is clean and cold, and therefore ideal for this type of space.

Dining rooms

The dining room is a space where the table and the diners are the main features; so the light should be focused on them. The most appropriate lighting is that which comes from above as it favors the food and creates interesting shines on the elements found on the table. The ideal light source for above a dining table is a hanging light –or two, if it is a very long table–. If the light is height-adjustable it will be even more convenient and if we may have to move the table to another place we should choose a light that can be easily moved. When we select the light for the dining room we must bear in mind that if the bulbs can be seen they may be bothersome, and when we install them we should be careful of their height so as not to bother the view of the diners.

We can complement the central lighting with a foot or table lamp. Candles are also an option worth considering in the dining room, as if placed on the table or a piece of furniture they can offer a warm, homely lighting, ideal for meals with family or friends.

Lounges

The lounge is the most difficult room in the house to light and requires the most efficient and versatile lighting. This is because it is a space where a wide variety of activities will take place: eating, speaking, reading, sewing, studying, watching the television... The ideal would be to achieve a lighting that was flexible enough to be adapted to each of these situations without any problem. This, however, is no easy task and may take time and some experimentation to achieve.

Hanging lights, which in the past were often used in lounges, are leaving these spaces in favor of the dining room. If we apply this type of light in the lounge, we will find that the light is insufficient and may cause bothersome shadows. This effect could be moderated using other points of light like foot or table lamps, but it would be preferable to have ambient lighting that is sufficient in the first place. To achieve good lounge lighting we should establish a double plan of action. We should ensure that we have generous ambient lighting that allows us to carry out general and

recreational activities. This lighting can be achieved using points of light located on the ceiling and walls, whether in the shape of ceiling lamps, spotlights or wall lamps, and whether direct or indirect. We should also plan task lighting that is highly flexible and suits each of the different activities: a foot lamp next to an armchair for reading or sewing, a table lamp on the desk for studying, a light on or next to an auxiliary table for informal meals and to watch the television... we are the ones who define the needs our lighting must meet. The combination of the two types of lighting will allow us to adapt it to all of these situations and over time it can be improved by moving or changing the elements it is composed of.

Finally we need to speak about lighting for decorative purposes, which can form part of the ambient lighting or be independent from this. Flush-mount lights, hidden behind a cornice, a spotlight that illuminates a sculpture or a picture, a wall bathed in light, the beam from a light projected onto the ceiling... are some examples of decorative lighting.

Bedrooms

Modern life has made us forget the traditional idea of the bedroom as simply a place where we sleep, to give way to a multi-functional and comfortable space, which reflects the personality of its owner. Above all a bedroom must be comfortable, a space that allows us to relax, but also a space where we can work, study, read, listen to music and keep personal objects, especially clothes.

Firstly, as with most of the spaces in the house, it is basic to achieve efficient ambient lighting. In this case we should be careful where we put the lights on the ceiling as they may bother us when we are in bed. Adjustable spotlights would be especially useful in this case, as they allow us to direct the light to areas where it is needed and avoid direct and vertical illumination of the bed.

Task lighting must be focused both on the bed, and on the other work or study area. To efficiently light the bed we can situate the lights on the wall or a bedside table, ensuring that the light can fall on a book and that the bulb does not blind us. In the case of the study area, a flexo table lamp would be the most ideal because it is easily moved.

An area traditionally forgotten is the dressing room or wardrobe, whose lighting is as important as that of any other room in the house. The light from the bedroom lights will not be strong enough to reach the interior of the wardrobes or beneath the shelves, so a special lighting should be designed for these features. There are light sources especially designed for this purpose on the market, normally with fluorescent tubes, as these give a cold light, which is more similar to daylight.

Studies and libraries

Studies and libraries are mainly work spaces, so decorative lighting takes a backseat in favor of a functional one. This does not mean we must forget about the former, just that the latter is more important. For study and reading spaces ceiling lamps are not the most ideal, as they cast bothersome shadows onto the work area. In this case our best resource are foot or table lamps, especially adjustable ones. This allows us to position them so they light up the work area correctly without a glare.

On the work areas, the light should arrive at an angle of 20 degrees or more, as if this angle is less, the light falls too low and produces bothersome, elongated shadows. We should be careful to avoid an excessively marked contrast between the work areas and its surroundings, as contrasts can tire the eyes.

When the functional lighting is sufficient and appropriate we can consider the decorative lighting, which will act as a complement to the former or in situations that do not require a specific work lighting.

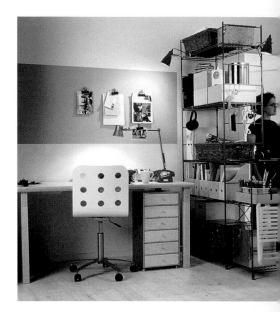

Top 10 Tips

1 We should be careful that the lighting of a stairway is practical and functional, highlighting the different planes that the stairs are composed of.

2 We should be able to activate the light switches in the passageways or on the stairs quickly and practically.

3 In the kitchen we should position task lighting above the work points. The switches should be away from areas with water.

4 Halogen bulbs are particularly ideal for the bathroom as they produce a clean and cold light.

5 The lounge requires a versatile and efficient lighting, able to adapt to different situations.

6 In bedrooms with work, study or reading areas, we should remember that this needs independent and adequate task lighting.

7 If we want an object to be the focal point of a space's decoration, we can achieve this by positioning a light to highlight it.

8 In libraries, studies or work areas in general, the lighting takes second place and practicalities take priority.

9 Outside the lighting must be both decorative and practical, with special attention paid to passing areas, paths and stairs.

10 The secret of good lighting is not based on a large amount of lights and bulbs, but on knowing how to find the most appropriate lighting for each of the spaces according to their needs.